W9-ABI-577

JEAN GIRAUDOUX
The Legend and the Secret

Jean Giraudoux (right) is warmly greeted by a spectator (identity unknown) in Vienna following the opening of his play *La Guerre de Troie n'aura pas lieu (Tiger at the Gates)* at the Josephstadt Theater. Annette Kolb translated the play into German *(Kein Kreig in Troja)*, and Max Reinhardt and Ernst Lothar directed the production. In attendance at the premiere were the Austrian minister of public education, numerous ambassadors, and seemingly all of Vienna. (6 November 1936)

JEAN GIRAUDOUX
The Legend and the Secret

Jacques Body
Translated by James Norwood

Rutherford ● Madison ● Teaneck
Fairleigh Dickinson University Press
London and Toronto: Associated University Presses

Translated from the French edition,
Jean Giraudoux—La légende et le secret,
© Presses Universitaires de France, 1986

Associated University Presses
440 Forsgate Drive
Cranbury, NJ 08512

Associated University Presses
25 Sicilian Avenue
London WC1A 2QH, England

Associated University Presses
P.O. Box 39, Clarkson Pstl. Stn.
Mississauga, Ontario
Canada L5J 3X9

The paper used in this publication meets the requirements
of the American National Standard for Permanence of Paper
for Printed Library Materials Z39.48-1984.

Library of Congress Cataloging-in-Publication Data

Body, Jacques
   [Jean Giraudoux. English]
   Jean Giraudoux : the legend and the secret / Jacques Body: translated by James Norwood.
      p.   cm.
   Includes bibliographical references (p.   ) and index.
   ISBN 0-8386-3407-9 (alk. paper)
   1. Giraudoux, Jean, 1882–1944—Criticism and interpretation.
I. Title.
PQ2613.I74Z5623413   1991
848'.91209—dc20   89-46424
                                                                 CIP

PRINTED IN THE UNITED STATES OF AMERICA

Contents

Translator's Acknowledgments   7
Preface   9

1. The Author-Character   17
2. The Limousin Utopia   31
3. The Eternal First   47
4. The Player   62
5. Feminine Singular   78
6. The Presence of One Now Absent   103

Conclusion   120
Notes   122
Bibliography   142
Index   149

Translator's Acknowledgments

The translator extends thanks to Dr. Maureen Wesolowski (Department of Modern Languages, St. Mary's College of California) for her expertise and many contributions to this manuscript, and to Dr. Agnes G. Raymond (Professor Emerita, Department of French, University of Massachusetts, and author of *Jean Giraudoux—The Theatre of Victory and Defeat*) for her excellent suggestions, which derive from a profound understanding of the writings of Jean Giraudoux. Without their assistance, this translation would not have been possible. Special thanks are in order to Professor Body, who took time to read drafts of the translation and, in numerous instances, to make additions to his original French manuscript for this American edition.

PREFACE

"Perhaps this writer, who is so discreet and self-effacing in his fiction, will some day speak to us about himself." Thus did a young philosopher in a turtleneck sweater—Jean-Paul Sartre—publicly challenge in the March 1940 issue of *La Nouvelle Revue française*, the most famous writer of his time, Jean Giraudoux, who was currently in front of a microphone in his capacity of Commissioner General of Information during the "phoney war" (1939–40), while the former was meditating in the weather bureau to which he had been assigned.

And the question is not a simple matter of banal journalistic voyeurism, nor of traditional biographical criticism. Let us see it in context at the very end of the article: "I would also imagine that a Marxist would call Mr. Giraudoux's views a rationalism of politeness, and that he would explain the rationalism by the triumphant rise of capitalism at the beginning of this century—and the politeness by Mr. Giraudoux's very special position in the heart of the French middle class: rural upbringing, Hellenic culture, diplomacy. I do not know; perhaps Mr. Giraudoux knows: perhaps this writer, who is so discreet . . . ." (etc.).

Giraudoux did not respond. He remained "discreet"; he continued to be "self-effacing in his fiction"—or to hide behind his fiction. Unless perhaps *Recollection From Two Existences*, that incomplete manuscript from the years 1940–42, could be the beginning of an answer? He died on 31 January 1944, before he could complete it. From that time on, there has been a Giraudoux mystery—or rather two Giraudoux mysteries, since there were two Giraudouxs: the public man and the private writer. The goal of the present essay is to build a bridge between the two and to provide a preliminary biographical sketch along with a study of the innermost sources of the work: perhaps the truth is not unworthy of the legend.

By what door shall we enter into the work of this author of such diverse literary genres: writer of tales and of short stories, novelist, essayist, journalist, screenwriter . . . and, above

all, dramatist? Yes, but even here, what variety: political and
sentimental dramas, classical tragedies, light comedies, fairy
tales, proverbs, fables, and often numerous genres combined
in the same play. . . .[1]

The simplest thing would be to start with a book: *Bella*, his
most classical novel, or *Tiger at the Gates*, his most celebrated
play; though some readers, Gide for example, fell in love with
the subtle music, the pointillist sketches, the sad and mocking
landscapes of *Provincial Ways*:

> Do not think that dead leaves fall all at once, like ripe fruit,
> or silently, like faded flowers.

> The careful oak trees, afraid of a downpour, draw their shadows
> around them.

> This was one of those landscapes which the shadows color sepia,
> which the dust powders over, which are rustically embellished,
> and which reflect your sadness as they send back the echo, softened,
> ironic, a bit foolish.

—Or rustically amusing: "A horse passed by. The hens followed behind, full of expectation." (Paul Claudel burst out
laughing at this and recommended the author—at the time a
junior vice-consul—to Philippe Berthelot, head of the cabinet
of the Minister of Foreign Affairs. "It is possible that I owe
my career to that," Giraudoux later reminisced ironically.)[2]

Proust adored "Night in Châteauroux":

> Along this walk, every step I took left footprints; the traces we
> leave in this world are deepest where our feet have trod most lightly.[3]

Valéry was "charmed" by *Simon the Pathetic*—by "this elusive
prose that arrests you":

> I preferred to know nothing about myself, and not to tear away
> from my eyes this blindfold, whose gentle pressure also bound the
> head of love against mine. It was an easy task. The days used to
> follow one upon the other, from sun to sun.[4]

Scholars love the Homeric pastiches of *Elpenor*:

> "O foreigner," asked Nausicaa, "who are you?" Elpenor stood up,
> offended:

"Ah! Excuse me," he replied, "you are the foreigner!"

Nausicaa softly said to him:

"And yet, Our guest, this is my country, my town; these trees are my trees!"

"That's exactly what I was going to say," responded Elpenor, "this is a foreign land. The scents with which you have inundated me are foreign scents. What do you call this tree?"

"The dendrodendron," said Nausicaa.

"You are not going to tell me that that is not a foreign name?"[5]

Both Michel Tournier and Marie-Jeanne Durry were dazzled by *Suzanne and the Pacific.*

Thousands of unknown birds were drifting around me like a new language. The entire island was ruffled by the slightest wind. Every time I raised my arms too fast, I seemed to be shaking out a red or blue carpet, and when I awoke and spread my arms to yawn, I seemed to be ripping it apart. The West wind wafted towards the ocean balls of fluff, which floated like toy swans on the lagoon until they reached the spot where the current took them and carried them, compacted into pillows, towards the Khouro Shiro. . . .[6]

Jean Anouilh, for his part, was possessed by the demon of the theater on the opening night of *Siegfried.* He was profoundly moved by the solemn voice of an amnesiac with a double name, a hero with two countries:

It would be absurd that, within a human soul, where the most contradictory vices and virtues cohabit, the word "German" and the word "French" alone should refuse to come to terms. I refuse to dig trenches inside my being.[7]

But more than one adolescent girl thrilled in unison with *Ondine:*

Oh, you aren't missing anything. By this very evening, you will be kissed. . . . But how sweet it is to wait. . . . Later, we shall remember this hour . . . the hour when you didn't kiss me. . . . This is also the hour when you didn't tell me that you loved me. . . . Don't wait any longer. . . . Tell me. . . . Here I am, with trembling hands. . . . Tell me.[8]

Jacques Robichez praises above all the witty lightness of *Amphitryon 38:*

Amphitryon. We shall live happily in our palace, and when we are very old, I shall obtain an extension from a god, so that he will change us into trees like Philemon and Baucis.

Alcmena. Do you think it will be fun to change leaves every year?[9]

But René Marill Albérès has pointed out a kind of metaphysics of purity, defined as "a distance with respect to humans, a brotherhood with creation," and this purity becomes the prerogative of women in *Sodom and Gomorrah:*

Everything about women is noise, distraction, and yet within them is the cage of silence, where the slightest creaking and the slightest palpitation of the world are perceived. Everything in them is egoism, flesh, and yet they are the sextant of innocence, the compass of purity. Everything in them is dread, and yet they are courage itself. Their eyes are blinded with mascara, stuck with false eyelashes, and yet they see what the angel sees.[10]

Shall we continue to enumerate those who favor, among the novels, *Eglantine, Juliette in the Land of Men, The Adventures of Jerome Bardini, Struggle with the Angel, Choice of the Elect?* As for the theater, those who swear only by *Judith,* or *Intermezzo,* who place *Electra* above all the others, a tragedy situated between two smiles, *Supplement to Cook's Voyage* and *Song of Songs*—not to mention *The Apollo of Bellac?* What shall we say then about *The Madwoman of Chaillot* and *For Lucrece,* his two final plays? One, ethnological, political, ecological, and antipsychological; the other, sentimental and feminist; both prophetic?

But then we hear a protest from the urban and rural league for whom Giraudoux is first and foremost the poet and pioneer of city planning in France, as can be seen in *Full Powers.*

Then there is the fellow Giraudoux scholar who will reproach me for not mentioning a minor work like "The Upper-Class Woman,"[11] and who will extract a necklace of iridescent pearls from the charming *School for the Indifferent:*

I see Madame de Sainte-Sombre's handkerchief, with her initials, like the wreck of a ship whose name is nearly obliterated; I see Miss Spottiswood, whose first name I don't know, like a big basket of flowers whose handles I am unable to grasp.

The moon is about to rise. Miss Spottiswood is walking silently alongside the evening. She is like a translation next to its original.

If I kissed this divine wrist, I could understand the singing of birds. If I touched these eyes with my finger, every color in the world would stand out separately.

The moon is about to rise. The birds are telling me:

"Go for everything that looks like what you want, Jimmy the Great, without closing your eyes."[12]

Must one choose? When one selects a book, one also selects an author. And then comes the reaction of Aragon, for a long time hostile towards Giraudoux and his "abuse of generalization," his odd images which grab you "like thorns on a bush":

> Yes. I had come to like that. All of it.
> That is why I lose my critical sense when reading Giraudoux; why I am touched by his faults as well as his strengths; by his errors, which bowl me over, by his seriousness in light matters, his lightness in serious matters.[13]

Yes. I had come to like that. All of it: as if a mysterious thread linked each volume to all the others, above and beyond the differences in genre, subject, and period. And what about style? It is often said that all of Giraudoux's characters speak like Giraudoux. That is not true: the rhetoric of the Rag Picker is not that of the President, and it has been established on the basis of statistical analysis that the style of his novels is not at all like that of his plays.* But it is true that each sentence bears a certain hallmark that makes us say: This is Giraudoux. A Giraudoux with a rich or limited vocabulary; a terse or eloquent expression; the different levels of discourse; multiple concerns; unexpected references; a constant need for renewal; an eye fixed on the great classics but an ear attuned to current events; indefinable and yet always himself; recognizable—recognizable from his style, perhaps, but style according to Proust's definition: a matter not of technique but of vision. Nothing common, and nothing too personal either: a slightly aloof way of being present; a sublimated eroticism; the art of juggling velvet swords with bare hands; a justifiable pride and the modesty of a Micromégas, presenting himself as a native of Bellac, on the planet Earth. This is how Giraudoux etched himself on plate glass for his narcissistic pleasure and for our own.

---

*Translator's Note: See chapter 3, note 20 for the reference to Etienne Brunet, *Le Vocabulaire de J. Giraudoux.*

JEAN GIRAUDOUX
The Legend and the Secret

1

THE AUTHOR-CHARACTER

"It has been said that I composed without corrections; this is true. I have only to let myself go, so why should I make any changes? My manuscripts are clean as a lily, as a window pane, as a virgin."[1]

A popular writer? He did not write for the "general public," although on numerous occasions, he flirted with the ambition or the illusion of doing so.[2] Nor was he a "popular writer" in the sense of writing what his readers were anticipating—"anticipated surprises," which are the essence of the novel according to Proust's definition—but at least he had "gone public" in one sense, that it had been a long time since he left the solitude of the Limousin or even the more populous cloisters of the lycée at Châteauroux. He had been famous in Khâgne at Lakanal and later at the rue d'Ulm.* For an entire year, he had been part of Munich society, another year that of Harvard. Nowhere did he go unnoticed. Beginning in 1908, he was a regular customer at numerous public places, such as the café Vachette, at the corner of the boulevard Saint-Michel and the rue des Ecoles. Around Jean Moréas gravitated Antoine Albalat, Paul-Jean Toulet, Curnonsky, Emile Clermont, André Billy, Jean de Pierrefeu, the brothers Tharaud, and others: a circle of literati, showing off and watching one another.

After the war, and even after his marriage, Giraudoux was also an habitué of the Deux Magots, Lipp's [a bar], occasionally the [café de] Flore, less frequently at Montparnasse "where he was a spectator more than an actor," observes André Salmon. For the café was a theatre, and in this literary café, what better role was there to play than that of the writer?

---

*Translator's Note: Giraudoux was a student at the Lakanal lycée and later the prestigious Ecole Normale Supérieure, located on the rue d'Ulm in Paris. Khâgne is the preparatory class for the Ecole Normale Supérieure.

A popular writer, since he wrote increasingly in public. When
he was at the rue d'Ulm or a little later, he would hide in
order to write and would then show his completed pages to
the incredulous Emile Ripert and Paul Morand: "I have never
seen anything like it!"[3] But later, Paul Morand saw him begin
Simon at the chateau of Feuguerolles in 1911; André Morize
saw him rewrite the same Simon on the deck of the ocean liner
La Touraine, which was taking them to the United States in
1917. His deputy in the Foreign Affairs press bureau during
the years 1924–25 more than once saw him ask for a stack
of paper on arriving at the office at ten o'clock and emerge
around noon with twenty pages filled. During rehearsals at the
Athénée, Jouvet had only to drop him a hint: "I do not know
what is the matter with Renoir today; he is having trouble with
his monologue," and Giraudoux, knowing what an irreproacha-
ble actor Renoir was, rewrote the monologue on the spot and
on his knee! Giraudoux scribbling is a spectacle that has often
been described: chest slightly bent forward, elbow resting on
the edge of the table, and hand suspended above the paper—a
spectacle immortalized in several photographs and by a very
great painter who was also his friend, Edouard Vuillard, in
a famous pastel that must date from 1931.[4] "I take a blank sheet
and I begin to write; the characters emerge as I go along; and
by the end of five or six pages, I have a clear picture in mind."[5]
He wrote while on vacation, for relaxation: a month of vacation,
another novel. And when he "went over" to the theater, he
would produce not in months, but in weeks. Every journalist,
of course, had his own bit to say. André Billy, for example,
who had known him for twenty years: "His profession was not
literature; it was diplomacy. He only worked on literature in
fits, once or twice a year, and he did not waste any time. Once
the first page was written, the first situation resolved, he had
only to let his pen run on, and his three hundred pages would
suddenly be covered without corrections."[6]

The proof is there: those clear, clean, full sheets. Those manuscripts, which are already passing into the hands of the dealers.
And so that no one should be unaware of it, the publisher
Lapina, in 1930, inserted in Fugues on Siegfried a facsimile
of the manuscript: two pages of "Divertimento of Siegfried"
placed side by side, containing a single correction on the left
page, a correction made on the same line; the name of a character
crossed out on the right hand page and replaced by another
one; and the remainder in a beautiful, rapid but clear handwrit-

ing, scarcely more careless by the end of the second page. In point of fact, however, this is a fabrication. And the entire beautiful legend of the public writer is false. Or more likely, like all legends, false and true.

It is a fabrication. In the collection of manuscripts of *Siegfried* that the author himself carefully preserved and even had Jeanne Lefranc bind attractively, *not a single* page—among thousands— was laid out in this way. Giraudoux always placed his sheet vertically; this one by contrast was taken horizontally, and folded in the middle to constitute two small pages side by side, as in a book. The text that it reproduces corresponds to the fifth of the successive typewritten versions and thus to a stage of the writing process at which (as had been his habit for quite some time) Giraudoux merely sent his text to be typed when it had accumulated too many corrections.[7] A false manuscript specially produced by Giraudoux himself—without any words crossed out other than those he chose—for the publisher's convenience and for the author's glory.

And what about the manuscripts of autograph dealers? When the young Jean-Pierre asked his father for spending money, the latter would occasionally take his pen and dash off a dozen lines that the child could cash in at the special dealers' in a neighboring street. A threefold gain: money for the son; prestige for this father who under the very eyes of his son was drawing gold out of the base lead inkwell; and finally, a source of glory for the writer without fear or error.

So the legend of the Knight Giraudoux, the Pierre Bayard of letters, is a hoax? And are these virginal manuscripts a falsification? And is this prodigious talent a lie? Better than a lie, the exact opposite of a lie: a creation. Not content with writing Giraudoux's works, Giraudoux created Giraudoux. Not only did he make himself, as self-made man and *homo novus*, but, among all his dreamlike creatures, he created his own image, perhaps the most beautiful of his works. Above all, he created this image of the nonchalant and productive writer: "When a word is dangling on my pen, I shake it out, from my lounge chair, into the lake. . . ."

For it is true that from the twenties on, Giraudoux became a prodigious writing machine. He left a considerable body of work: sixteen plays, sixteen novels, five essays on sports, literature, and politics; two screenplays, and dozens of other articles yet to be collected. A considerable body of work, especially for one who had led a career as a civil servant as well, with certain privileges to be sure, but who lived only three years after retirement—three years that were his most productive. Even apart from these years of retirement, one notes an increasing productivity, as if it became easier and easier for him to write, and as if he had been telling the truth when he said to those close to him that writing is an easy matter, and, in particular, in spite of the commonly held belief, that writing for the theater is easy.

On the other hand, certain individuals playing the connoisseur—the foremost among them being André Gide—will tell you that the best Giraudoux is the early Giraudoux, the Giraudoux of *Provincial Ways*. Now, *that* Giraudoux did not find writing easy. Up to and including the war years, he left rough drafts, unfinished and scattered, but obviously reworked, scored out, written over. The "writing machine" is not really well-oiled until the period of the novels in the twenties, beginning with *Suzanne and the Pacific* (1921) and *Siegfried and the Limousin* (1922), producing one novel per year during a month-long vacation and, later, producing one play plus another book each year, not to mention articles.

It is true that the manuscripts of this period are sparsely corrected, written in a regular and supple handwriting, occasionally even "clean as a lily, as a window pane, as a virgin." The blank page, which inhibited so many other poets, stimulated Giraudoux. By what mystery? That is the Secret which we seek above all to unlock. But truthfulness obliges one to admit that the neatness of these manuscripts is less mysterious than it might appear. René Marill Albérès, in studying the *Origin of Jean Giraudoux's SIEGFRIED* (Minard, 1963), followed by Colette Weil in her critical edition of *Intermezzo* (1975), and finally the Pléiade edition of the *Complete Theatre*, have supplied the first reason, which is no longer any secret: Jean Giraudoux was a tremendous recopier, rediscovering the work habits of the very good pupil that he has described in *Simon*.

First of all, he conceptualized prior to writing. See Simon and his "sheets of narration, scattered but already numbered, like the stones of a building." One should not suppose that he already had a plan, that he knew the episodes that were to lead to the dénouement even before he wrote the first line. On the contrary: "In this way, without forethought, I begin to write at random. . . ."[8] Instead of a plan, he has an outline in mind, a trajectory along which he could guide his pen; more a matter of *wanting* to write, and *knowing how* to write than *knowing what* to write. Knowing how to write as one knows how to swim, to dive into water: "Every morning, I merely used to push to one side the books, letters, and torn envelopes that piled up inevitably, on the white board from which one dives into my memory."[9]

In the second place, he worked over his manuscripts as Simon worked over his notebooks: "I had a big, neat handwriting, notebooks with a double margin, the kind in which corrections did not become a degrading blotch, but a variant, an appendix."[10]

In the third place, rather than scoring out too much, he would rewrite, but not in the childish way that consists of rote copying. Let us suppose he had an earlier draft in front of him. Relying on his memory, having in his head the previous version, as well as a plan for altering it, he would rewrite the episode, the chapter, the scene while virtually hoarding his earlier inspirations, but disposing them along a new course.

Writing was for him a sport. He often prepared for it during one of the "long hikes" that were customary for him. When he arrived at ten o'clock in his office after unknown detours,[11] and completed an entire chapter in a single sitting, it is conceivable that he had been going over its itinerary in his mind in the course and to the rhythm of his walk. The art of Giraudoux, which has occasionally been called affected and over-elaborate, consists on the contrary of incorporating the *pizzicati* of existence into the *continuo* of the narration. The most remarkable thing is that his manuscripts contain blanks, later completed in a different ink: to keep the rhythm, he would avoid struggling for a word that would not come, and went ahead with what came easily. As he said in *Electra:* "Happiness was never the lot of the laborious."[12]

Pierre Bressy, who was a very friendly colleague of Giraudoux's in the press bureau at the Quai d'Orsay, explained the Giraudoux phenomenon in terms of the ideal that their generation had cherished: the ideal of developing a personality, free of specialization—a development of both the body and the spirit, a harmony of spirit and body. This ideal was to restore the balance, the golden mean, the wisdom of the Greeks. Giraudoux belonged to that generation of new Athenians of which Coubertin was the most famous strategist (but one should also mention the Hébert method, the College of Athletes, and Dr. Carton). A member of "La Lycéenne," an athletic club at Châteauroux; a university champion of the 400 meter dash;[13] a rugby and football player (the Sunday morning games were highlighted by the speeches of a veteran player named Charles Péguy); a tennis player at Saint-Amand-Montrond, with his Bailly friends, while at the Quai d'Orsay with Philippe Berthelot. He was accustomed, until the 1914 war, to begin his day with a session of gymnastics (which took place in the artist's studio of Paul Morand's father), and, until the 1939 war, to frequent swimming pools and beaches, and, as a spectator, the Princes' Stadium. Throughout his life, he maintained a brisk gait, an easy bearing, and a lithe figure.

The volume *Provincial Ways*, marked by a pre-athletic sensibility (postsymbolist, neoimpressionist, decadentist? or does it really matter?), collects disparate specimens of a chilly, fearful, myopic, and awkward humanity. After his visit to America in 1908, Giraudoux becomes a novelist with broad shoulders, who leads his characters and his readers through marathons, and turns his intentions outward, filling his pages with oxygen. In an even more direct way, Giraudoux entered sports journalism in the 1930s, publishing more than ten articles or prefaces under this rubric. Better still, in *Full Powers*, he emphatically called for a "program of French hygiene." Sports, then, along with city planning, took the place of politics for him. For a long time, he had boasted of reading only magazines (*L'Echo des sports* and *L'Auto*). In *Full Powers*, he writes that "sports are democracy . . . , aristocracy . . . , energy . . . , courtesy."

The small volume entitled *Sports*, issued by Hachette in 1928 in a collection of "Notes and Maxims" is startling, first of all, in its form.[14] The maxim is not solely, as the first publishers suggested, "experience in a nutshell, wisdom in capsule form." It is the athletic record of the writer; it sums up in an instant his years in training. The cover of the first edition already asked the question: ". . . but, for Jean Giraudoux, isn't literature the leading sport?" And one could indeed state that his art consisted of taking hurdles in his stride, and timing his rhythm in such a way as to "keep his lead." At the time, he was pursuing a four-fold career: he had been champion in the stadium; he had acquitted himself well during the war; he was a diplomat (the supreme Career); he was a writer. Theater, city planning, politics, and cinema were going to double the number of careers he pursued by turns.

Thus, writing for Giraudoux was one hygiene among others, one ambition among others, one success among others, singled out only because the others were reflected in it. "Inspiration," which he had believed in since his time at the lycée, came to him from a global image of himself.[15] The words of Buffon, "Style is the man himself," acquired a rich meaning. And the writer is himself more important than what he writes, as Giraudoux would later explain à propos of Charles-Louis Philippe, his neighbor in the tiny town of Cérilly, whom he observed for hours on end through a window: "The spectacle of the writer filled me with much more emotion even than the reading of his works." An enemy of masterpieces—those "statues of literature" which "clutter up its avenues"—and opposed to the "specialization of the man of letters," Giraudoux had the sole intention of generating the "energy from which the creativity of tomorrow will blossom."[16] He went so far as to say that "writing is an accident in the life of the poet."[17]

As we know, the accident occurred and took on intrusive proportions after Giraudoux's meeting with Bernard Grasset, that athletic champion of publishing.

The regulars at the café Vachette, as elsewhere, were richer in manuscripts than in publishers. One may judge the state of publishing at the beginning of the century from the doctrine of the very distinguished Alfred Vallette, founder of the *Mercure de France*: "I never do any publicity for the works that I edit. When they are bad, it is quite useless to do anything to save them. When they are good, then they will command attention on their own."[18] In accordance with this doctrine, publishers limited themselves to one modest printing; a second edition signalled a great success. Young authors could only wait, manuscript in hand. Bernard Grasset was the one they had been waiting for. Wealthy not from having won at the racetrack, as has long been suggested, but from a modest inheritance (3,000 francs) and blessed with a faith worthy of that of Bernard Palissy (whence the absence of furniture on the fourth floor at 49, rue Gay-Lussac), Grasset transformed the room that he was sharing with Louis Brun into the headquarters of the *Editions Nouvelles*.* The two friends selected manuscripts, negotiated with printers, took care of mail, and kept the books. Grasset visited the principal bookstore outlets, presenting himself as his own

---

*Translator's Note: Bernard Palissy was a celebrated chemist who, it is said, burned all his furniture to keep his kiln going.

agent: a heroic pioneer, a legendary *self-made man*, who, in order
to succeed, was forced to invent, or at least to introduce, *mar-
keting* into French publishing.

The publisher at the beginning of the century, recounts Grasset, "was content with printing the work, announcing it in the
old booksellers' newspaper, giving complimentary copies to the
press, and waiting for orders." Grasset would completely change
those practices: he increased the number of complimentary copies, for which the bulk of the first edition of *Provincial Ways*,
which hardly sold, was used.[19] Offering a high discount, indeed
a very high discount (33 percent, or 40 percent for more than
fifty copies) to the bookstores, auctioning off books himself at
the gates of the ancient theater of Orange, he also sought and
found foreign outlets: Brussels, Amsterdam, Geneva, Lisbon. Finally and most importantly, he advertised. His philosophy was
that people read what is being read. One needs only to persuade
them that a book is selling in order for them to buy it. And
so he announced in his 1911 catalogue that a given title was
in its sixth edition—when it is known that of the first printing
(one thousand copies) only eighty had been sold at the end
of seven years! This is an extreme case and almost farcical,
but one that explains why one month after the appearance of
Siegfried and the Limousin, Louis Brun asks Jean Giraudoux
to "be good enough to consent to the next printing beginning
with the 80th edition instead of the 39th!"

Grasset was able to implement his policy in full only after
the success of *Maria Chapdelaine*, launched very conscien-
tiously in 3,000 copies to inaugurate in April 1921 the collection
of "Cahiers verts" in literary circles. It subsequently was given
free of charge, in series form, to *L'Action française* in exchange
for an article by Léon Daudet, promising "immortality," no less,
to its author; and later distributed in an inexpensive edition
with the revolutionary goal of having *Maria Chapdelaine* read
"by every Frenchman." Every means would be used: the press,
politicians, Canadian ministers, booksellers, a committee that
placed a plaque in the author's native home, Franco-Canadian
rapprochement, a stage version of the novel, a literary survey
("What does the success of a book depend on?"), a competition
organized by the Maritime League, brochures to administrators
and college professors, not to mention the infinite number of
rural pastors charged with offering *Maria Chapdelaine* "to an
individual particularly likely to enjoy it" and who became, in
their pulpits, the naive and, consequently, all the more effective

propagandists of an unprecedented publicity campaign. Bernard Grasset was able to boast of having reached in one year an unheard-of printing of 600,000 copies, fictitious of course, but in reality surpassing 150,000, which was in itself unsurpassed.[20]

Nevertheless, it would be unfair to consider Giraudoux the product solely of Grasset's techniques—in the first place, because Giraudoux had not waited for *Maria Chapdelaine* to make a name for himself. At this time, he already had two publishers and Grasset had to compete with Emile-Paul Brothers for him. He had not even waited for Grasset to slip some short stories first into student journals, then into such respected journals as *Athéna, L'Ermitage, Le Mercure de France, La Grande Revue.* Nor had he waited to become the right-hand man of the redoubtable Bunau-Varilla, director of the *Matin,* for whom he was personal secretary prior to being placed in charge of the Short Fiction column.[21] Better still: while the literary circles were being manipulated by Bernard Grasset, Bernard Grasset was being manipulated by Giraudoux. One was an actor, and the other was an actor and a half. But why talk of actors? These were two artists, two accomplices, two friends who succeeded the one because of the other, each in his own domain.

The correspondence of Grasset and Giraudoux reads like a masterpiece of English humor. What clearly emerges is that Giraudoux knew how to play his part to perfection. Grasset was irremediably seduced. Not content with publishing his *Provincial Ways* and with giving him an advance (at the time, he was publishing Proust at the author's expense) although sales had not nearly equalled his expectations, Grasset contracted to pay Giraudoux a series of monthly installments, to which Giraudoux countered very amicably with a request for doubling one of those installments. Then Grasset offered him a fixed monthly salary for reading and evaluating five or six manuscripts per month: the salary would remain fixed even if he had less to read. The deal was completed, and after the first report was submitted, there was a glowing letter of acknowledgment from the publisher, who sent another manuscript accompanied by an urgent letter, for the publisher had an appointment with the author; next an alarmed reminder, also unanswered; next a letter of accusation; next . . . guess what? Another glowing letter of acknowledgment. After weeks of silence and negligence, Giraudoux had only to present himself, speak his piece, put on his little act, and Bernard Grasset would again be babbling protests of friendship, admiration, and gratitude. And this would last until Giraudoux's death. Between the two wars, Grasset, who was involved in the longest psychoanalysis in the history of psychoanalysis (so they say), often left to Louis Brun, who became his "literary director," the job of dealing with Giraudoux; and Louis Brun reacted with greater resolve than his boss had been accustomed to do, dictating to him, "in the presence of five people in the firm who all take an interest in the eternal life of the work of Jean Giraudoux and in the transitory life of the house of Grasset," a letter in which he amicably wrote: "You don't give a f. . . about the house of Grasset."

As a matter of fact, it is clear from the letters of Louis Brun that Giraudoux treated his publishers in a most offhand manner, accepting advances on a book that he never wrote or that he brought to another publisher, signing with Emile-Paul for the publication of his complete works and with many other publishers for luxury printings, notwithstanding earlier contracts with Grasset. In the archives of the rue des Saints-Pères, one may thus find a veritable chain of reminders, reprimands, and threats, followed by a note from Giraudoux: "Wire monthly check to P.O. Box in Nice." As Louis Brun once wrote to him, he was treating his publisher like a banker.

An example? For the rights to his next novel, Grasset had already paid Giraudoux sums that were considerable for the time and above all for a young writer who was not selling at all, only to find out that Giraudoux had given his first war memoirs, "The Return from Alsace," "The Day in Portugal," "The Grand Tour," "Dardanelles," and "The Five Nights and Five Reveilles of the Marne," to Emile-Paul, who then brought out *Campaigns and Intervals* (1917). Whence these two letters dated 15 and 16 November—both of them from the publisher to the writer. The first one ends on the word "betrayal" and expresses "grave reservations" concerning the financial consequences. The second begins as follows: "My dear Giraudoux, Out of modesty, I do not wish to mention the complimentary things we said to each other this morning, following your delightful visit, and I shall limit my remarks to letting you know all the satisfaction that I am feeling. . . ."

Giraudoux had not needed to write. All he had had to do was to show up, and Bernard Grasset completely reversed his position. In fact, Giraudoux "had" Grasset "where he wanted him," in a sense, and he knew that he did: Bernard Grasset did more than bet on Giraudoux to win; he had invested considerable sums in his name with the hope of future gains. If Giraudoux got away from him, he would lose his investment. It would therefore be better to concede to him a supplementary monthly payment, better to increase his fixed salary, better to close his eyes to his temporary lack of loyalty. But the more he invested, the more dependent he became, and the more Giraudoux demanded—with a charming and promising smile. However, Grasset for his part knew what he was doing. "Our profession, as you know," he wrote to Giraudoux on 22 February 1922,

> is a profession in which it is necessary to have foresight, and in which we can no longer think in terms of one book at a time. In view of the effort that the promotion of an author requires and the advances that we are obliged to offer him, we need to have the assurance that his fate is truly tied to ours. You know, too, the extent to which my means have been stretched and that I now understand as well as anyone, it seems to me, how to produce a success.

This final reference to *Maria Chapdelaine* explains why Grasset was proposing to Giraudoux a "general contract," binding him "at least for the next three novels" he would write, and why he was pointing out that he could now make him an offer as good as that of Emile-Paul, and indeed worth "much more than his." "I can [promise] one thing that he would not endeavor to achieve (since he makes no effort on your behalf), and that is to win a large audience for you."

Giraudoux accepted. Grasset sent him the general contract for three novels (while leaving Giraudoux the possibility of fitting in another novel, between the second and third, to the profit of some other publisher). Thus was announced the series of *Siegfried and the Limousin* (Grasset, 1922), *Bella* (Grasset, 1926), *Eglantine* (Grasset, 1927), despite the slight difference that *Juliette in the Land of Men* (Emile-Paul, 1924) was added not between the second and the third, but between the first and the second; and in spite of the fact that the "general contract" had been annulled in the autumn of 1922—at the request of Giraudoux, who may have had scruples after *Siegfried and the Limousin* had won the Balzac prize, which, as was only too well known, was a creation of Grasset's.

Bernard Grasset taught Giraudoux that one does not publish one book, then another book, then a third, each of which would have its own function, each of which would find its own readers, as if they were by three different authors. In twentieth-century publishing, the public expected from an author not a book but a career. The first book rarely brings in a profit, and is only the foundation of an edifice destined to evolve as a result of a series of complex operations that are aimed less at the literary critics and the publisher than at the reader, as Jean Giraudoux clearly stated when he insisted on paying homage to "literary advertising" the way his publisher practiced it:

> I saw the birth of the house of Grasset, in which I was one of the first authors, and I often appreciated the energetic manner in which Bernard Grasset circumvented the hurdle of the critics in order to present the book to the reader. The conviction of a publisher that he has a fine book should indeed suggest to him all the possible ways of persuading people to read that book.[22]

The publisher gets people to read one book. It is up to the author to get them to read the next one; to satisfy the reader's curiosity while arousing in him an even greater curiosity. The faithful reader is often faithful to a routine. Giraudoux, on the other hand, went out of his way to change genres: *Provincial Ways, School for the Indifferent, Campaigns and Intervals, Simon the Pathetic, Elpenor*. Each is likely to confuse the readers of its predecessor, unless Giraudoux's art consisted precisely of confusing, surprising, and establishing "new associations among things" with an agility which inspired in Proust "the admiration which an awkward boy who gets nought for gymnastics feels when he watches another more nimble."[23]* His readers, it is claimed, began to flock to him only after he had produced one war story after another (*Campaigns and Intervals, Amica America, Adorable Clio*); fame began with the series of novels (from *Suzanne and the Pacific* to *Eglantine*); then glory, with the series of plays. In this very period, however, Giraudoux was expressing his wish, having finished one work, that the next one should be very different. Though confused, his first readers were caught in the trap of seduction and intrigued by a style, a voice, and an author of which they knew nothing. Gide begins his review of *Provincial Ways* by saying: "Nothing could be more youthful" and concludes it suggesting that the

---

*Translator's Note: Trans. C. K. Moncrieff and Terence Kilmartin, *Remembrance of Things Past*, vol. 2 (New York: Random House, 1981), p. 338.

author "had left his early youth behind."[24] From book to book, the author portrays himself as a larger-than-life character hidden or divided up among all the others. A hint of autobiography hovers over every detail that is slightly probable, and the improbable itself is taken as a metaphor of the real. The hidden author may even betray himself in a place name, in an object, or in an adjective. Besides, Giraudoux would avoid strict autobiography, which gives the impression of scrupulous and dusty research, but he would gladly play puss-in-the-corner with boys of his age, who would grow old along with him. Let us take as an archetype the narrator of *Siegfried and the Limousin,* who is given the first name of Jean (just as the narrator of *Remembrance of Things Past* is called Marcel) and who is two years older than Siegfried, who is thirty-seven. Jean is thus the same age as Giraudoux when he wrote his novel during Easter 1922, and rewrote it in the month of August—without having experienced the adventures narrated in the course of an action that begins very explicitly in January of 1922. The book would appear just in time to receive the Balzac Prize on 28 October, the day before his fortieth birthday—an exceptional coincidence and a cunning intervention by providence, but which suggest a model for the infinite possibilities of subtle confusions and planned interferences. On condition that the author appears around town, not completely identical with, but at least equal or parallel to the way he appears in his books: naturally artistic, humorous, and omniscient. The effect produced by the work combines with everything else revolving around it and around its author in the diverse channels of fame.

For the main thing was to make a name for oneself, figuratively and, most of all, literally. The student at Châteauroux, dreaming of reconciling his peasant ancestry with epic and chivalric ambitions, liked to sign his name Gérald Houe of Bellac, taking as his motto: "By the sword, by the pen, by the hoe."[25]* The use of the pseudonym, so common to those who separate their real lives from their imaginary creations, was actually, for him, in the beginning no more than a brief temptation, in the years 1906–7—when he signed with discreet affection, Jean-Emmanuel Manière. Then it became a necessity during the even shorter period in which he was on the staff of the *Matin,* in compliance with the rule imposed by the director, Bunau-

---

*Translator's Note: The word *houe* is a play on words in French, denoting "hoe," and is impossible to render in English.

Varilla, on all of his employees[26]—J. E. Manière was then revived, soon to be replaced by Jean Cordelier (why he chose the name of Cordelier will be discussed later). But he signed Jean Giraudoux in 1904, on his first published narrative, "The Last Dream of Edmond About," later reissued under the eloquent title of "First Dream that was Signed"; he signed Jean Giraudoux in 1908, when he made his first appearance in the table of contents of the *Mercure de France* and *La Grande Revue*, just as he did in 1909, for his first book; and again in 1910–12, for the short stories that he gave to the *Matin* and to the *Paris-Journal*, which did not have very great literary pretensions.

In these onomastic variations, the first name survived. According to the office of vital statistics, as a matter of fact, he was called Hippolyte Jean. He unloaded this first legal given name onto such ridiculous supernumeraries as Robineau Hippolyte-Amable in *Siegfried* and Jean-Hippolyte, Baron Tommard in *The Madwoman of Chaillot*. At home, at school, at the lycée, as in his diverse careers, he went by Jean, and it is believed that this first name was given to him by his mother. Perhaps a clue comes from a line in *Simon*: "She called me by a name that she had chosen, that my father had disliked, and which was not my own."[27] However, his paternal grandfather was already named Jean Giraudoux. This name, which has a certain music and a certain savor, but which had only been heard in the farmyards of Lower-Limousin, he would bear in the city as well as in the bookstores, and bear it with a proud smile, in obedience to the admonition of Simon's father in the very first page of *Simon the Pathetic*: "Your grandfather was a peasant. There have been neither accountants, nor wig makers, nor horse traders between you and him. You can make of your name what you will; it is new; it has never appeared on a shop sign, nor on the paper that lamb chops are wrapped in. Be thankful for all these privileges, and put down that apple."

2

THE LIMOUSIN UTOPIA

Is the Limousin in the title of *Siegfried and the Limousin* a man or a province? Is it the narrator who accompanies Siegfried on that long return to the native land that concludes the book, or is it their native land? No one will ever know: Giraudoux loves these ambiguities. Compare, for example, how in "Echo," one of his earliest short stories, the word *clarinette* occasionally denotes the clarinet player (who sits upon the parapet) and occasionally the clarinet itself (which can attain a high pitch)— "and one subsequently knew what a *clarinette* is all about."[1] One knows what the Limousin is about, be it the man or the province: the poorest thing there is in France; providing Paris-Moloch in the previous century with its tribute of immigrant workers. The soil of the Limousin is barren for everyone: "The only soil in France which is composed throughout all of the same rocks. Every unarmed Limousin gives out the same sound over the entire expanse of his province."[2] As for the culture of the Limousin, it has been known since Rabelais by the burlesque stereotype of the Limousin school child.

A paradoxical pride: for want of blue blood and forebears, a very distinguished diplomat, a cherished writer, the glory of Paris, will make it a point of pride to remind us that he is a native of an unknown little town named Bellac, and that he learned French in the school of the natives of Limousin. Better yet, he boasts of being doubly Limousin, on his father's side and on his mother's, and he even boasts of having been doubly Limousin for generations: "As far as one could go back into the history of my family, one could establish that it had never left Bellac."[3]

These genealogical considerations are reminiscent of the period when the Spanish Inquisition suspected Marranism of anyone at court who had a Jewish ancestry. Since mixed marriages had taken place in commercial towns, there could be no better proof of nobility, in order to cut short any attacks on one's "honor" and to establish the "purity of one's blood," than to be able to point to four quarters of rural ancestry. But such smiling claims to autochtony have their unpleasant underside: the tendency to racism, which is difficult to exorcise. Raised in the school of French nationalism, Giraudoux was to speak at first of "the Jews," making use of the banal and offensive epithets that were current throughout the French countryside. Then, as he made the acquaintance of ind: vidual Jews, he was to feel the desire to know them intimately and to depict them— just as he was to feel the desire to know and to depict those Germans who had originally been introduced to him as his hereditary enemies. He never knew the convention, established immediately following the Holocaust, that consisted of denying any specific Jewish trait, of avoiding even pronouncing the word *Jew*. The *Reflections* of Sartre *on the Jewish question* having established that that which constituted what is Jewish in the Jew was the fact that he was the *other*, one no longer had to know or to say who was Jewish, nor what this might signify for him or for others. Today, on the contrary, Jewish traditions, Jewish thought, Jewish humor demand special consideration for themselves, which Giraudoux in his own time gave them. He did not consider the assimilated Jews to be Jewish. However, he characterized those apart from the national community as do certain doctrinaire proponents of Judaism who are opposed to assimilation. He denied them neither his curiosity—Moses in *Eglantine* may testify to that—nor his admiration. *Judith*, inspired by a Jewish actress (Elisabeth Bergner), performed by another Jewish actress, in the theatre of Baron Henri de Rothschild, is the proof.[4]

Perhaps it is necessary to give Giraudoux credit for not having uttered the word *Jew*, so uniformly shouted down in the official speeches of the period, when he brought out in the spring of 1941, at the instigation of his brother, that *Message to the Legion* wherein he paid the Vichy regime the minimum tribute that he believed was required of him in order to play with the slightest outcome for success his trump card of city planning (of which we shall speak again).[5] Nonetheless, the word "purging" linked to the idea of French "race" several months after the statute regarding Jews had been enacted demonstrates that Jean Giraudoux had committed a sin of levity, if not a lapse in lucidity or courage. Still, he must not be condemned without an attempt to understand his thinking, which is presented at greater length in *Full Powers*.

A quick reading of the chapter that deals with "The Population of France," otherwise called "the French race," might lead to a hasty—too hasty—accusation of racism, with citations to support it. Giraudoux's "racism" has nothing to do with the racism that was raging beyond the Rhine during the same period and that was met, in France itself, with consent and complicity, scandalously exonerated today. (Isn't that so, Céline?) Giraudoux even sought an antidote to it. He was not dreaming of "creating in its integrity, through purification, a primitive, physical type, but of constituting, if necessary with foreign influx, a moral and cultural type." One could say today: adapting immigration quotas to the limits of employment and to the needs of the economy, defining a policy for population, and unifying the optimum conditions for sociability. But Giraudoux was imprudent enough to speak aloud about the problem of naturalization, a problem that political parties prefer to eschew even today. His friend Pierre Bressy, who presided over the Commission of Immigration, provided him with naturalization figures for the years 1935–37, for his articles in the *Figaro*. These articles were the basis for the lectures of 1939, collected under the heading *Full Powers*. Giraudoux denounced the unfair privileges and the lack of consistency in the office of naturalization: "With a mean of 2,500 Polish naturalizations, although we have fifteen or twenty times more Polish farmers and miners than Poles in other jobs, 2,200 city-dwellers were naturalized, of whom 1,500 were Jews. And they will be the first ones to be naturalized." Today, one cannot read these words without feeling uneasy, for one cannot help thinking about what followed. One wishes that one had nothing worse to read on the subject. Yet the sequel demonstrates first of all that it was not a question of anti-Semitism: ". . . they will be the first ones to be naturalized. Freud, should he wish to become a Frenchman, will have to wait. Waiting for fifteen years have been renowned scientists, art collectors who promised to donate works to the Louvre, managers of factories who have proven to the nation that they are fully capable of becoming our citizens. For them, whether they are Aryan or Semitic, despite continued exertions on the part of myself and my friends . . . , no single consideration will be given to their valor, their dignity, their service."

Above all, it is essential to distinguish naturalization from immigration, and to distinguish the act of bestowing French citizenship from the act of offering asylum. On this latter point, Giraudoux, far from sharing the xenophobic instincts of the French right, commended France as "the only civilized nation where there is immigration": "Since the League of Nations has not yet been able to create the country where one might for a time find shelter from all the demons of the century, demagoguery, tyranny, and the severity of prejudice," he willingly accepted that France should be this nation. He could not read the too-well-known formula *France for the French* "without experiencing a nasty shock": "I am not a foreigner. My mother was from the Lower-Limousin, my father from the Upper-Limousin, and their union, although it was considered at the time by both families as a slightly exotic alliance, could not possibly have conferred upon me a nationality that was subject to question. It seems to me, however, that in these words, one of my most precious rights is being contested, that a limit is imposed on one of the senses by which I live."[6] And more precisely: "This phrase, *France for the French*, instead of enriching me, dispossesses me." These antixenophobic pronouncements are not simple words of caution. In any case, Giraudoux seems to have changed since the day in 1919 when he was asked to participate in a survey in the journal *Littérature* of which we shall speak again in the following chapter.

To the question: "Why do you write?" Giraudoux did not answer the question and responded somewhat crudely: "I write French, being neither Swiss nor Jewish." A humorous response, as the sequel confirms, but which concludes with the evocation of his supreme title: "Born in Bellac (Haute-Vienne)."[7] For, this child of the secular schools, who owes his emancipation and his ascension to the mastery of the French language, has repressed the memory of the local or regional dialects and does not mention them except as an item of folklore. At the turn of the century, the Occitan dialect stopped several kilometers from Bellac, and survived, at best, among the elderly and the least educated classes—a patois which his mother, on the other hand, had completely shaken off; she did not even have what Giraudoux calls "that Midi accent which my father reverted to when he became surprised or upset."[8] By tracing his ancestry from Bellac, Giraudoux chose his mother's country and repudiated his father's. For his father's country was Chirac; it was Liginiac, the Corrèze. Bellac, however, was not merely his native town; it was the country where his maternal grandfather, veterinarian by profession, practiced his trade, and was also the birthplace of his mother; of his maternal grandmother, Marie Gouat; of his great-grandfather Gouat; and of the great-grandfather of this great-grandfather; and even of the father-in-law of the latter, named Jean Mingeard, born around 1687, who could have been the grandson of La Fontaine, as we shall see.[9] In his education, in the shaping of his literary sensibility, Jean Giraudoux was above all his mother's son. Bellac was the land of his mother and his motherland, and French was his mother tongue. Even his first book, *Provincial Ways*, invites us to Bellac: "In Bellac, enter, if you please, the house where I was born, and, looking down from the third floor, you will have to admit, whether you like it or not, that this is truly the most beautiful town on the face of the earth. . . ."[10] In fact, the young Jean Giraudoux would not have had the slightest recollection of the home of his birth, as his family was obliged to leave it when he was just a year old. Because his father, who had been working for the highway department in Bellac, decided to go into the administration of finances, the family embarked on an itinerary from one tax-collection to another, thus acquainting the author with "the Bellac-Bessines-Pellevoisin-Cérilly-Cusset circuit which no Cook's tour anticipates."[11] His mother had a brother and a sister. The brother—Giraudoux's uncle—settled in Saint-Amand-Montrond (hence his interest in Cérilly); the sister married in Vichy (hence his interest in Cusset). After the death of the grandmother, the widow of the veterinarian, in 1897, Giraudoux's parents had no more relatives in Bellac, had no further reason to return, and never did. No doubt Jean Giraudoux would pass through there—even making an occasional detour in order to do so—when he went to visit a female cousin in Sornac, when he went to Limoges to the Havilands, and when he returned via Yzeures-sur-Creuse to see the other Havilands and his childhood friend, Suzanne Lalique. But one may say that when he began to write the name of Bellac—that is, when he began to write—the real-life ties to Bellac had been totally and definitively broken. This is where the myth of Bellac begins. Little by little, Bellac will take its place in the writer's personal mythology as he passed it on to his readers, the legendary capital and center of concentric circles that expand outward to the province, to France, to the planet, and to the cosmos.

The first time, the myth of Bellac takes the form of poetic fantasy. The Homeric episode of Ulysses and the sirens is well known. Giraudoux turned it into an ironic tale, in *Paris Journal*,

in 1912. He would make use of it again in *Elpenor* in 1919.
Their ears plugged with wax, the sailors shout like deaf men,
and consequently Ulysses hears nothing of the song of the sirens.
But he does not wish to disappoint his companions and begins
to improvise a poem, which he himself recites prior to declaim-
ing it:

> "Of Bellac, I descry
> the melancholy abbey,
> the Avenue and that lake
> (which is not there!).
>
> And I see besides
> autumn in person,
> blowing a horn
> that does not sound;
>
> The summer's fair
> and Aunt Solange,
> hating the visitor
> who does not eat;
>
> My youth withal,
> which—God knows lacked charm!—
> wrenches from my cold heart
> this tear!"[12]

School for the Indifferent had just been published; this brief
tear squeezed out of a cold heart confirms it. Giraudoux while
bidding adieu to his "charmless" youth and to its melancholic
landscape, was having fun—with "that lake which is not there,"
"a horn that does not sound," and "the visitor who does not
eat." A bit of Laforgue having fun.

The second time, the myth of Bellac takes the form of bucolic
description. One should reread the entire first chapter of *Suzanne and the Pacific*. Thus Suzanne, prior to setting out for
Australia, the Pacific, the shipwreck, and her anti-Robinson destiny, has had a childhood and an adolescence that were inseparable from their setting. This setting was Bellac—that is, to be
exact, the series of houses that are lined up south of the Palace
Square and the rue Thiers, noble façades of granite with wrought
iron balconies along the street, a small garden to the south,
and a panoramic view of the valley of the Vincou and the sur-
rounding countryside. Did the veterinarian grandfather live in

one of these houses? If not, what Bellachon living there welcomed a visitor named Jean Giraudoux? An observant visitor,
as the description of Suzanne indicates:

> Each French window faced onto the town, each window onto
> a landscape of streams and hills, with fields and chestnut groves
> like patchwork . . . , for this was a land that had already been well
> used; it was the Limousin. On the days of the fair, I had only
> to turn around in my chair to no longer see the marketplace, and
> to discover the countryside emptied of its flocks. I had grown used
> to making this half-circle at any opportunity, seeking, for every
> passerby—the priest or the sub-prefect—his counterpart of empti-
> ness and silence within the hills; and to change the realm of sounds
> was scarcely any more difficult; I had only to change windows.
> On the street side, some children playing train, a phonograph, the
> hawking of newspapers, and the kid goats and ducks that were
> being carried to the kitchens, uttering a cry that became more and
> more metallic as it became their cry of death. On the mountain
> side the real train, the moaning and the bleating that in winter,
> one could sense even before hearing it from the vapor surrounding
> muzzles.

For the evocation of the still very rural life of this end-of-the-
century, for the description of strolls in the neighborhood; the
return home with black currants, strawberries, and raspberries;
barefooted adventures in the stream; the sounds of day and
the sounds of night ("one could hear, according to the season,
soft or hard plops on the ground: it was the apricots or the
nuts falling"), for "every quivering poplar, every rushing stream,
every belated wood pigeon" that offered itself and grew within
us "like a metaphor," the Bellachons will perhaps forgive Suzanne and her author for having said that their town was situated
along the national highway from Paris to Toulouse—at best a
secondary route. A local historian has also taken him to task
for having praised the charms of the Promenade du Coq. For
really, only a Bellachon from Paris could confuse the "Promenade," which is one thing, with the "rue du Coq," which is
another! But I have been assured that in addition to the rue
du Coq, which still exists, there used to be below the church
in Bellac a balcony overlooking the Vincou, decorated with a
cock that by now has flown away.

Giraudoux would never again risk describing Bellac so mi-
nutely. He calls it by name in Siegfried and the Limousin (1922).
He evokes it in Intermezzo (1933) and will speak of it again

at length only to revive his faraway past, particularly in the context of the episode of Jean de La Fontaine, which merits scrutiny.

The third stage in the myth of Bellac plunges us into history and legend. In "Visit to the Prince," an episode drawn from the early drafts of *Siegfried and the Limousin* and published as a short story and then republished with other short stories in *Sentimental France,* the narrator, addressing a prince of the ancient German nobility, describes the Limousin as an island: "It was on its banks that Young had seen the first green lizards. It was on reaching its shores at Chalus that Richard the Lionheart had received an arrow right in his heart in the midst of the chestnut trees, and Jean de La Fontaine, while entering the haven of Bellac, in the midst of the poplar trees, had received a less cruel arrow from the hand of my great-great-great grandmother." This fleeting allusion he develops in a lecture of 1932, "Tragedy of Yesterday and Today," which, reworked, will appear in 1941, in the volume *Literature* under the title "Bellac and Tragedy."

> Recently, convinced that every township in France had its Periclean age—for I have experienced it myself in two of them—I wanted to research that of Bellac. . . . An era of grandeur . . . to which the great men of France were led (one knows not by what route, nor would they ever have occasion to travel it again) to pass through Bellac, whether they were called Henri IV, who saw an eclipse there for the first time; La Fontaine, who, thanks to my great-great-great grandmother, conceived his fable of the *Stage-coach* there; or Fénelon, who claimed to have been received there by the Limousin schoolboy himself.

The episode of Jean de La Fontaine, already mentioned twice, will be elaborated finally in the prelude to *The Five Temptations of La Fontaine.* Giraudoux recounts that at the lycée

> the idea came to several of us to claim that we were descended from famous poets. . . . A series of extraordinary family ties was established between the little Berrichons named Godard, Baty, Laprade and personages who were better known, even at Châteauroux, called Corneille, Lamartine, or Musset. . . . As for me, I was unlucky: I was born in Bellac. . . .

He proceeds to explain that the only two poets mentioned in the local chronicles were Jean Tournois and Victor Gonjoud:

Such ancestors could not satisfy my ambition. . . . I learned that two great writers had stayed in Bellac. There lay my salvation. All that was needed was for these writers to have known my great-grandmothers and to have loved them, and been loved by them, and I was saved. . . . It was soon clear to me that for one of these writers, I did not have to bother. He was an archbishop, he was Fénelon, and he was the "swan" of Cambrai. . . . Of the second traveler, one could expect better things. True, he had stayed in Bellac for only a night, but this was Jean de La Fontaine, who knew how to make good use of his nights, and legend had it that he stayed in a house near that of one of my great-great-great grandmothers. That one of my young relatives should have suddenly recognized in this guest a great poet, rushed to him, joined with him in a secret marriage, is precisely how boys in junior high school picture to themselves passion and poetry, and it was not out of the question, either, for the renown of the family, that La Fontaine, for his part, had experienced a sudden and irresistible attraction. Besides, that was possibly what really happened, in any event.

Giraudoux was not the antirealistic writer that has been suggested. In the geographical index of his works (an index that is yet to be drawn up, just as the complete works are yet to be published), the actual settings of his life occupy a privileged position. The Pacific of *Suzanne and the Pacific* and of *Supplement to Cook's Voyage* remain the only *terra incognita* of any importance, the only land that he discovered *after* having described it. The rule is that he sets the action of his novels in the places that he knows. At the top of the list in number of appearances, Paris is well ahead of Munich or Harvard, ahead of Châteauroux, and even ahead of Bellac. Yet Bellac is a reference point right up to that *Apollo* which he had entitled *of Marsac*, and which became *of Bellac* without anyone's knowing exactly how. But all the little towns in which he lived during his childhood and his adolescence are included in his magical geographical lexicon. The hero of "Mirage of Bessines" spent his childhood in Bessines. The narrator of "Sainte-Estelle," in *Provincial Ways*, recounts how he used to play at the home of the local woman who was miraculously cured, that Estelle Faguet or Faguette on account of whom Pellevoisin (Indre) is even today a place of pilgrimage. Cérilly also lived its Periclean age, if one is to believe "Visit to the Prince," and Saint-Amand-Montrond is the subject of a report in *Pages of Art* (1919), prior to its appearance in *Siegfried and the Limousin* as the last capital of French mysticism.[13] Thus there is no county seat or village

in which Jean Giraudoux lived but he made himself *ipso facto*
its poet and historian. In a different direction, leaving Bellac
occasionally to orbit around the monument of Bruère, that
sarcophagus-like milestone where the novelist used to curl up
as a child and which marks the center of France,[14] the circle
continued to expand from the "periphery of the Limousin" to
the "center of Auvergne." From Aigueperse (*Juliette in the Land
of Men*) to Charlieu (*Eglantine*), a Massif Central is sketched
out, a central France, which has produced, according to "Visit
to the Prince," Montaigne, Pascal, Montesquieu, and then, if
one is to believe a certain article on Charles-Louis Philippe,[15]
Jules Renard, Valery Larbaud, Charles-Louis Philippe, and (by
implication) Jean Giraudoux. A country of streams on whose
banks the story of *Juliette* begins and ends, rivers that run
through the French compositions inserted in *Siegfried and the
Limousin*, compositions that foreshadow the lesson that will
be recited by the little girls of *Intermezzo*:

> "The Creuse flows into the Vienne, the Auron flows into the Cher,
> the Sioule flows into the Allier . . ."
> "No, the Bazine!" I shouted at you.
> "What river does it empty into?" you replied, for you were hoping
> at least to come up with a name that was well known.
> "Into the Vincou," I shouted again.
> "But what about the Vincou?"
> "In the Gartempe."
> "You are stubborn; especially when you are naked."
> "But what about the Gartempe?"[16]

It was up to the author of *Siegfried and the Limousin* to
take the names of these streams and conduct them to glory.
The narrator visiting the prince explains that the Limousin is
water, and that civilization consists of playing with water:
bridges, locks, fountains—a civilization that is steady, motion-
less, and profound like a pond, the symbol of human memory.

It is time to dive in. Here, from the same work, is the return
of Siegfried to his native Limousin. Here Giraudoux revives
a device that Proust made famous at the end of *The Captive*,
describing the itinerary of the little train that takes the narrator
from station to station and from memory to memory, crossing
through the strata of memory in an order as chaotic as geological
beds.

"The name of the first Limousin train station was called out, and suddenly this *département* that I had left at age two and that I believed I did not know welcomed me as its child." There follow names of stations—stations or villages that will never have a station master and a station outside of this narrative— at the whim of a most fanciful itinerary: Argenton, Saint-Sébastien, Azérables, Eygurande, La Souterraine, Gargilesse, Crozant, Rasé, Morterolles, Bessines, Le Breuilh-au-Fa, Droux, Ambazac, Fursac, Blond, Rancon, Fromental, Larsac, Le Raynou, Saint-Sulpice-Laurière, Montagnac, Ambazac, Magnac-Laval, Le Dorat, every name tied to a memory,

> and the infallible appearance of each anticipated name—Look, there is Droux, Pierre-Buffière is not far off—close to that creature who no longer possessed either his father's youth or his own—Look, Folles and Bersac have disappeared; no, there they are!—gave me, even more than the indication of a successful experiment, the only true measure that I have found—yes, there's Bellac!—of the human condition.[17]

Such is the fable of all of Giraudoux's accounts, always recurring anew. It starts in the peaceful family haven, in the bed of the boarding school, in the union of the couple, in the peacefulness of the village, and the harmony of the province. Then comes the unexpected arrival of the stranger, man or woman, adventure, religion along with its gods and its angels, culture with its big words, politics with its great ambitions, imagination with its phantoms—sowing desire, doubt, uncertainty, misunderstanding, war, revolution, often even death. A perfectly reversible analysis: all one has to do is write and the stuffy air of all-too-human rooms is suddenly purified by a cleansing wind from the mountain tops, from space, from other worlds.

Each flight ends with a return, be it humorous or tragic (it hardly matters) to the point of departure.[18] Whether it be Suzanne or Siegfried, Juliette or Eglantine, Bardini or Edmée, Judith or Isabelle, Florence or Ondine, every man and every woman returns to the ranks. All come back to their places, but they come back different, changed by what they have seen on the other side of the front or the border, beyond the river or the ocean, beyond human existence.

"The customs officer who opened the gates of Geneva to me when I was twenty was the first foreigner I had ever seen, except for two Parisians who visited for a funeral, and vanished at the same time as the deceased."[19] The lecturer of "Tragedy of

Yesterday and Today" is only barely joking: a Parisian in the little world of his *Provincial Ways* really was a foreigner, and, conversely, every provincial on the evening of his arrival in Paris had the impression "of having abandoned and having killed."[20] Paris—the Exhibition, then the lycée of Lakanal— marked his first flight out of the central France which had sheltered his youth. It was in 1900, and he was about to turn eighteen. And he was about to turn twenty-one when, on leave one Sunday toward the end of his military service, on another excursion, he went to Geneva and crossed his first border. Facing the lake, he wrote to his parents: "The sea—or almost."[21] His father had never seen the sea and he was often teased about the fact that "the greatest body of water" that he had ever seen was the pond at Sagnat.[22]

"To escape! To escape far away!" will be one of the persistent temptations of the writer from Limousin.* First of all, to flee boarding school: "To hear the name of a town when one is in boarding school, a prisoner, is to make a vow to get to know it."[23] Next, to flee the university: "They wanted me to be a professor? Fine, but not until the age of sixty, or possibly fifty-five; first I wanted to go where their Latin and their history would be useful to me—to travel."[24] To flee France; that is why the young student of the Ecole Normale Supérieure abandoned literature to "leap into the Germanic"[25] and obtain a student scholarship that allowed him to spend a year in Munich from May 1905 through April 1906. Even that was not enough. He arrived via Belgium and Holland, and for his first summer, he left Munich for a long tour of Austria, Hungary, Bosnia-Herzogovina, and Italy. The following summer he visited Northern Germany, Denmark, Berlin, Dresden, and Prague, this time by car with his friend, Louis Bailly from Saint-Amand-Montrond, until he was able to boast: "My tenth country."[26] In 1917, Paul Morand charted his travels on the planisphere with a blue pencil; Giraudoux added his own in red pencil. "He was very proud," recalled Morand, "to beat me by 2,000 kilometers." It must be said that, not content with having received a scholarship to Harvard when he left the Ecole Normale Supérieure, Giraudoux was named junior vice-consul, then vice-consul at the office of research in the Foreign Press, so that before the war,

---

*Translator's Note: This citation is from the poem "Brise Marine" by Mallarmé, trans. Anthony Hartley, *The Penguin Book of French Verse* (Harmondsworth: Penguin, 1951), p. 425.

he had on numerous occasions escorted the diplomatic pouch to Moscow or Constantinople, and that subsequently he "took advantage of" the war to fight in the Dardanelles campaign and then, after his second injury, to leave on a diplomatic-military mission to Portugal and to the United States, while Paul Morand, on a special assignment, was shuttling between London and Paris. Later on, Morand caught up with him and greatly outdistanced him as the expert traveler he had become. With the war over, now married and a father, Jean Giraudoux showed himself to be much more the homebody. Several assignments in Germany at the end of the war; a trip to Rabat in 1923, on which occasion he was introduced to the sultan as "the Poet of the Ministry of Foreign Affairs"; a trip to Greece in 1930; two stays in Berlin in 1930 and 1931—the time seemed to be over when he would cross borders for pleasure. He told his colleagues: "If I were offered an ambassadorship at Versailles, I would refuse it: it's too far from Paris."* And indeed, when in 1924 Poincaré appointed him secretary to the ambassador of Berlin—a very conservative punishment, if indeed it was a punishment for him since it is usual to send a diplomat to a foreign country, and what better capital to choose for the author of Siegfried and the Limousin?—he no sooner reached his post than he asked for sick leave, after which he managed to obtain a new assignment in Paris in the press service. Giraudoux was to accomplish the feat of having spent his entire career without ever having been assigned to a post abroad. It is true that from 1934 on, while keeping the Quai d'Orsay as his port of registry, he again followed in the footsteps of Paul Morand. Having been named Inspector of Diplomatic and Consular Posts, he was in the Near East in June 1935 (Mosul, Baghdad, Tehran, Tabriz, Haifa, Jerusalem, Jaffa) and in northeastern Europe in December (Kaunas, Riga, Tallinn). In 1936, Central America and the East Coast of the United States in the spring (New York, Puerto Rico, Santa Domingo, Cuba, Panama, Guatemala, Mexico, Los Angeles, San Francisco, Vancouver: more than four months of leave, during which he drafted The Liar, then The Gracchi); and central Europe in the fall (Vienna, Budapest, Belgrade). Finally, from mid-October 1937 to mid-March 1938, he traveled around the world (New York, New Orleans, San Francisco, Honolulu, Auckland, Sydney, Bali, Batavia, Singa-

---

*Translator's Note: This information was conveyed to the author by the ambassador Pierre Bressy.

pore, Bangkok, Hanoi, Colombo). "Very far, too far; this is the
last of my long missions," he wrote to his mother.[27] But, in
spring 1939, he would have to leave again for two months in
the United States (New York, Chicago, San Francisco). He had
lost his taste for long excursions and during the Occupation,
he would leave France only to dash off to Lisbon in search
of his son in September 1940, and for a round of lectures in
Switzerland in the month of February 1942.

The rare seasons that he spent in France did not pass without
travel. The end-of-the-year celebrations took place among family,
often with his mother and brother, in Cusset. Easter vacations
took him to Savoie (Talloires), Roussillon (Céret), or Switzerland
(Vevey); summer to the beaches: to Honfleur or La Baule in
the twenties, to Nice, Cap-Ferrat, Cannes, or Biarritz in the thirties, and he always planned a stop on his return trip to spend
time with his mother. Even in addition to his vacations, he
continued to escape: a few hours walking through Paris or a
few days by car along provincial roads, first with his wife or
his son, or both, but more and more often alone—as far as
we know. Why, for example, would he telegraph Louis Jouvet
from Arras on 16 September 1935: "Impossible to return today"?
Why had he gone to Arras? That will be discovered farther
on.

In his travels near and far—and this is perhaps the most important point—the Limousin writer tamed landscapes, animals,
people, and sought everywhere the same complicity, and triumphantly acclimated himself under diverse skies. He would have
his friends, his creature comforts, and his routines in Munich,
in Berlin, in Boston, and in New York more truly than in Bellac,
as on his way through there with his son one evening, knocking
on Charles Silvestre's door and finding the "old glory" of the
place had gone deaf, he headed to Limoges to find a hotel!
In Vienna in 1936, everything charmed him: "There I rediscovered my theatrical and romantic Munich and Berlin, which,
incidentally, can no longer be found anywhere but there."[28] As
for America, it inspired him with filial sentiments, for each
time he set foot on American soil, he rediscovered his youth:
"Every time I return to eat my griddle cakes in Boston, my
mince pies in Albany, my prunes in Santa Catalina, they have
for me the flavor of the past that the Galician from Chicago
finds in his jellied carp when he makes his pilgrimage to Lvov.
America is my old continent."[29] Let us again travel through New
England and *School for the Indifferent*, Bavaria and *Siegfried*

and the Limousin, Central Park in New York with Stephy, and
California in Choice of the Elect: the Limousin utopia requires
that no land be a land of exile. The most beautiful illustration
of this is not to be sought in the last of the long missions
of the inspector general. Rather it is in the first novel that he
had written with a female title character, which recounts how
a young girl born in Bellac is shipwrecked on an island in
the Pacific and discovers there the most benevolent and luxuri-
ous nature, a nature which was itself feminine in its predilection
for luxury.[30]

"My native town is Bellac, Haute-Vienne," the lecturer pro-
claims at the start of "Bellac and Tragedy." Is there any reason
to be embarrassed about it?

> I shall not apologize for being born there. Nor shall I apologize
> for not having known a large city until I came of age, and for
> having spent my youth in only five towns, of which not a single
> one exceeded five thousand inhabitants. The benefits of this appren-
> ticeship have been incalculable. In sum, I was never less than $\frac{1}{5,000}$th
> part of the human agglomerations in which I lived, and, on two
> occasions, I was no less than $\frac{1}{1000}$th.[31]

Simon the Pathetic had declared to his aristocratic girl friend:
"You love me because my youth belongs to me, a genuine youth,
drawn from the countryside and from old books."[32] From this
youth—not merely provincial, but rustic—combined with reading and culture, Giraudoux extracted precisely the opposite of
a regional literature. Using his village belltower as the measure
for all the world, he, like Siegfried, "watches those dials which
mark the hours of all worlds."[33] The author of Siegfried a nation-
alist? As Robert Kemp and Georges Pioch observed at its first
printing, the play posed, more clearly than the novel, the question of fatherland, of nation, of race, and resolved it by excluding
both the nationalistic solution and the racial solution:[34] "That
invisible garment which is woven for an individual by his way
of eating, walking, and greeting; that divine harmony of flavors,
colors, and scents perceived by our childhood senses: these
constitute the true fatherland."[35] The author of Intermezzo a
regionalist? To be sure, the action takes place "in a country
of sandstone and porphyry," where one can see the "mountains"
of Blond, and Le Dorat is not far off. In the definitive text,
the name of Bellac was deleted, so that this little Limousin

town would become the quintessential small town and would
be studied from the perspective of Sirius, for even in a fragment
of the rough draft, the Inspector, who comes from Limoges,
told the swooning Isabelle: "You are on the planet Earth, my
child, satellite of the Sun, and more precisely, at Tilly in Bellac,
in the Limousin. . . ."[36] From this point of view, the unity of
the human species may be seen more clearly. Our Limousin
writer a racist? Ask him to define happiness: "Happiness,
Gladys, is harmony among all men, with every one, including
the Negro, to be considered among the greatest."[37]

3

THE ETERNAL FIRST

"You're going to the lycée to learn how to not let your time slip away. Every evening in bed, repeat to yourself that you are capable of becoming President of the Republic. The means is simple; you have only to be first in everything; and you have done that very well up until now."[1] Thus spoke the father of Simon, and thus Simon acted accordingly, always placing first in his class not only at his provincial lycée, but also when a headmaster from Paris offered him a place in his lycée. "At that national examination where all the students in France were asked to recreate the world according to their own aesthetics,"[2] he also won the prize, eternally the first.* This Legend gilded like the prize books of that era, Giraudoux illuminates with humorous quips. To the naive reader and to the short-sighted critic, who may confuse the author with his characters, Giraudoux appears henceforward as the eternal first: that fits very well with "those *for the first time* which grace all of his objects!"[3] It suits him so nicely! And besides, isn't it only the truth?

In the course of the year 1919, Jean Giraudoux, still poorly recovered from his combat experiences, was visited by three young men, themselves also severely affected by the ordeals of war, and who had just founded a journal, *Littérature*. These three young men were named André Breton, Philippe Soupault, and Louis Aragon.[4] The latter had just published in *Sic*, the prewar journal founded by Pierre Albert-Birot, a lyrical book review of *Simon the Pathetic*: "Despite your companions, Simon, I shall call you SOLITARY STROLLER." All four shared the view, developed later in "The Prayer On the Eiffel Tower," that

---

*Translator's Note: The *concours général*, or national examination, takes place in the final year of the baccalaureat, when the best students of different lycées write competitively on the same topic for honors and distinction.

the war had sounded the end of reason as Renan knew it. Did
they commune with one another in evoking the names of Nerval,
Rimbaud, and the German Romantics? Whatever the case, if
the three young men spoke to their elder about automatic writing,
they could only have encouraged him to give free reign to his
talent! But if the word *surrealist* was pronounced à propos of
The Breasts of Tiresias, the "surrealist drama" by the late Apolli-
naire, which had been performed in 1917, it was not by the
future surrealists, who were not yet using this label, but by
Giraudoux: as early as 1918, it seems, in a classification of contemporary French writers, he listed his name—all alone—under
the rubric "surrealist."[5] Consequently, one could consider in
the light of surrealism the response that he made, in December
1919, to the survey in the journal *Littérature:* "Why do you
write?"

> I write French, being neither Swiss nor Jewish, and because I have
> in my possession all my diplomas: Grand Prize of honor from the
> Lakanal lycée (1904, an excellent year), First Prize at the national
> examination (1906, an equally good year). *Licence ès lettres*, with
> honors. Graduated first in my class from the Ecole Normale Su-
> périeure. Born in Bellac (Haute-Vienne).

One might almost consider this to be a dadaist provocation,
were it not for the friendly relations among Giraudoux, Breton,
and Soupault. In his first chronicle in *Feuillets d'Art* (May 1919),
Giraudoux had made mention of the recent creation (in March
1919) of the journal *Littérature*. In the following year, *Littérature*
printed a prepublication chapter of *Suzanne and the Pacific*
and, according to the account of Benjamin Crémieux, the Dada-
ists made much of it.[6] The provocation was thus Giraudoux's
doing, and it was a double provocation. Beyond the nationalistic
and anti-Semitic remark, worthy of a partisan of the *Action
française* with his beret pulled down over his ears, the connection peremptorily drawn between the diplomas obtained long
ago at the university and his mastery of language today resembles a caricature of academic ideology and even resembles a
caricature made by Giraudoux in a lively sketch—for he drew
well—entitled "The Prize Winner." In it, a tall, husky boy stag-
gers under the weight of his awards and his laurels.[7] Certainly
Jean-Pierre Giraudoux was not mistaken in saying that his father's only snobbery was academic snobbery, and even after
he was a well-known writer, he did not refuse to join the associa-

tion of winners of the national competitive examination, nor
to preside over the awarding of prizes at his former lycée, nor
to address the former students of Châteauroux at banquets. The
eternal first is at once a naive picture and a caricature, each
having Jean Giraudoux as signatary and hero.* As for knowing
how to interpret the litany of honors that he exhibited in his
response to *Littérature*, it might be well to examine it more
closely.

Despite the fact that he had received a diploma while under
the minimum age requirement, and "at the head of the list,"
like the narrator of *Siegfried and the Limousin*,[8] the little scholarship recipient did not adjust without difficulty to the curriculum
of the lycée. Only Latin was a success right from the start.
He was not awarded a single first prize in the seventh grade;
he would have to wait until the tenth grade to accede to excellence, and, then, he would be on his way. His first year at
Lakanal presented equal difficulties in adjusting, which were
only resolved after he had repeated the year. It was in 1902,
and not in 1904 or 1906: at the same time that he was awarded
first prize in Greek translation at the national examination, he
was accepted at the Ecole Normale Supérieure, the thirteenth
out of twenty-one candidates.[9] This rank was not acceptable
to his pride and might explain in part why after having passed
the *licence ès lettres* (with the mark of "Good," not "Very Good"),
he switched to German, where the competition was less intense.
He was overcome by lethargy, a kind of torpor, a "difficulty
of being" that points to the difficulty of not being first, perhaps
a crisis of vocation as well. His dissertation completed, it is
said, with the help of several chums, received only the mark
of "Fairly Good," and the following year, when he took the
examination for the *agrégation* in German, he did not even pass.
Now the only graduation examination on the rue d'Ulm is for
the *agrégation*.** Under these conditions, the indication "Came
out first from the Ecole Normale Supérieure" has a comical
undertone for those who know the way in which the relations

---

*Translator's Note: The translation "naive picture" is a loose rendering of
"une image d'Epinal," which was a special kind of French popular imagery
known for its bright, gaudy colors. Its context here would imply something
naive and crude.

**Translator's Note: The rue d'Ulm is the location of the Ecole Normale
Supérieure, one of the *Grandes Ecoles*, or highly select and competitive schools
in the French educational system. The *agrégation* has no equivalent in the
American system.

between Giraudoux and the university had concluded. The humor is even part of the folklore of the Ecole Normale Supérieure from the time when Jean Richepin (class of 1868), having actually been expelled, rented a booth in the neighborhood with the sign of "Jean Richepin, came out first from the Ecole Normale Supérieure." (Legend has it that within a week he was reinstated.) Giraudoux's chums did not take offense: Didn't they know him above all as "a likable eccentric?"[10]

It is best to avoid all misunderstanding, for these considerations run the risk of appearing petty and even false: A Giraudoux incapable of making a good and honest academician? First, there is a reason to be thankful for it. Giraudoux possessed "the fantasy that the humanities depend on,"[11] and indeed much more than they could tolerate. Such can be said to be the nature of his "incapacity."[12] Moreover, one could challenge the legend of the eternal first with the best conscience, for the details presented here (or, rather, presented again, for they have already figured for ten or twenty years in scholarly studies) will not prevent tall tales from circulating and triumphing, thanks to agents both willing and unwilling. The significance of first places is in the eye of the beholder. Giraudoux was right to make fun of them. Obsessed by their educational system, French journalists and critics of Giraudoux's life have chosen to remember only those who place first. And even to the point of adding to them, and orchestrating the song of the eternal first as Chris Marker did on the first page—naturally—of his *Giraudoux by Himself*, "first committed writer," "first of the first," "first in his class," "first at the competitive examination, in his graduating class from Normale, at the competitive examination of chanceries. . . . First writer to be decorated."

Since Chris Marker has embellished the legend, we may be allowed to continue to dot the "i"s. Giraudoux received the Legion of Honor and the Military Cross medals after his second injury (21 June 1915).[13] Others had deserved it before he— notably Charles Péguy.* Giraudoux flunked the "comprehensive examination" for diplomatic service, flunked brilliantly. Having passed the written exam, he was, in the subsequent oral tests, the first one to be failed, this after preparing for them hastily and late, while still struggling to earn a living. Having reached the age limit, he could not take the examination again and had

---

*Translator's Note: Péguy, a brilliant young writer cut off before his prime, was killed in 1914.

to fall back on the "short examination" called "examination
of junior vice-consuls" or "examination of the chanceries," in
which he did indeed place first, but which he could have failed
with impunity, as he could have been admitted on the basis
of his diplomas alone. He acceded to the grand cadre and to
the "Career" only on the basis of the result of the "examination
of reclassification," or "examination of the demobilized" in
which he was ranked second.[14] This was in 1919 when he was
thirty-seven years old, precisely the year of the survey in the
journal Littérature. He was careful not to add to his university
honors the slightest mention of his diplomatic honors.

The "deceitful" declaration in Littérature (1919) follows immediately the publication of Simon the Pathetic (1918). Thereafter, Giraudoux would no longer need to lie. It would be enough
for him not to deny anything and to perpetuate his legend
through a discreet allusion to "memories left by [his] studies"[15]
or by a story which is transparent to anyone: "He was . . .
intelligent—the examinations of the Ecole Polytechnique are not
infallible proof, but if you are ranked first upon entering and
first upon graduating, no one can call it a coincidence."[16] He
pushed coquetry in "The Prayer on the Eiffel Tower" to the
point of saluting his former instructor at Châteauroux in the
following terms: "It has now been twenty-two years, Jules
Descouture-Mazet, since a similar springtime, when you hauled
me up to that tower for the first time, in my lycée uniform,
in order to give me on the eve of the national examinations,
the view of this city, which you claimed would be at my feet
should I place second in Greek translation." It is left to the
best informed readers the pleasure of clarifying that he was
awarded not second, but first prize in Greek translation, and
to the envious to add that this was not in the course of his
studies at Châteauroux, but two years later, at a time in which
students of "advanced rhetoric" were still competing with their
juniors!

In fact and without reservations, Giraudoux was intelligent.
That was the first impression that many retained of him. Not
only was he intelligent; he was "intelligence itself," the "record
holder of Intelligence," as he will be described in Je suis partout
immediately following his death, to implicate him more deeply
in having been the "minister of Propaganda of the Jewish
gang."[17]* Beyond a doubt exceptionally gifted among the lycée

---

*Translator's Note: Je suis partout (I Am Everywhere) was a Nazi-oriented students of Châteauroux, he found himself in Paris vying with others who were exceptionally gifted in France, and the more unfair rivalry of those among them who were, in addition, "heirs," of sorts, having been surrounded by books and bathed in culture since infancy—a struggle and a rivalry that were terrible for his pride. At the lycée of Châteauroux, he had finished triumphantly. From Lakanal, he left with honors. On the rue d'Ulm, he seems to have renounced rather quickly the option of doing battle. Fantasy is also a defense and an escape mechanism: it seems likely, judging from the ridicule which he repeatedly heaped on the *agrégés* and the academicians, that Giraudoux, whose vocation it had been to be eternally first, harbored as a result of failures some rancor of which he purged himself by drawing up this "surrealist" list of honors. His transfer from the school of letters to the school of Germanic studies and his movement in the direction of diplomacy undoubtedly point to a need for escape and, perhaps, already to the ambition of being above all a writer. These moves are also, however, for the eternal conqueror, acts of side-stepping, evasive maneuvering, and, finally, strategies of failure: failure at the German *agrégation* and failure at the "comprehensive examination" of foreign affairs. They are failures against which he had armed himself by alleging modest tastes, a failure that he disguised in recounting the Parisian career of *Simon the Pathetic*: "My teachers believed unanimously that I would become a teacher. One more examination, and, from student, I would be promoted to master. . . . I recoiled. Student today, professor tomorrow!— one night, one solitary night for everything in life that was not teaching!"[18]

What is certain is that Giraudoux had, with respect to the French language, the conviction that he was its master—an impression confirmed once and for all on the day when the professor of advanced rhetoric at the Lakanal lycée, handing back term papers, had scolded the class: "Gentlemen, there is only one student among you who knows how to write French. . . ."[19] When some former schoolmates pointed out to him numerous errors in orthography and solecisms in the printed text of *Bella*, he was visibly shattered. He recovered, and in *The Paris Impromptu*, he charged Jouvet with proclaiming that his characters

news publication that appeared during the Occupation (1940–44). Cf., Agnes G. Raymond, *Jean Giraudoux—The Theatre of Victory and Defeat* (The University of Massachusetts Press, 1966), p. 17.

"need all the nuances of our grammar and our language in order to explain their thoughts." In fact, an examination of his manuscripts reveals that Giraudoux made errors in French just like everyone else, except the pedants who cannot agree even among themselves about the final subtleties of agreements and license. To be in possession of one's language, in Giraudoux's case, takes on a broad and fruitful meaning. To be in possession of one's language is to have it at one's disposal, to nurture it, to enrich one's vocabulary with provincialisms and with neologisms, to bring the written syntax closer to the spoken language, to play freely with synonyms and with levels of language in order to increase the means of expression. That is, to combine the traditional French of villages and trades with the vocabulary of the sciences to give names to flora and fauna, materials and forms, to add to technical terms, as in sport, phoney technical terms. Mixing and embracing as it does civilizations, corporations, and administrations, Giraudoux's language, when placed in the memory bank of the computer of the Treasury of the French Language, appears richer than that of all his contemporaries.[20] The enrichment, from one novel to another, is itself exceptionally high—until the moment when Giraudoux, turning to the theater, began to practice, on the contrary, an economy of means, a narrowing down to a few key words, to veritable asceticism. Eternally first, that is, even for the dictionary?

From this legend will emerge three truths.

The eternal first was beyond a doubt the eternal student of the lycée: a product of culture, with an erudite allusion ever at the tip of his tongue, but also a bantering schoolboy who made fun of teachers and of his own erudition, cultivating pastiche and anachronism. As Cocteau put it: "A very good student who added to this virtue the mysterious prestige of the lazybones."[21] Concealing his effort, the student advertised his laziness, and succeeded in the only way which was both excusable and foolproof—by genius.

> I believed, like my whole class, in genius; for us, talent was of no account. . . . What is only talent, is disclaimed in the provinces! But we knew by heart all the famous lines of poetry and all the sublime quotations. How sweet is the sublime for a child reading, his homework done, in the poorly lit study hall, a rumbling storm outside. . . . But the sublime contains something bestial and pitiless

that I cannot describe; I preferred genius to it. I would become
tender and indolent when I contemplated genius. A mist hovered
over my thoughts, my first wrinkle appeared on my forehead. Why
hadn't my father, in a fit of madness, made a statue or a discovery?
It would only have taken a week! Or why didn't I have a genius
for a grandfather. . . ?[22]

This hereditary genius he would create for himself in romantic
fiction when he wrote *Bella* in the first person, evoking his
father, his uncles, and the entire Dubardeau family; a free transposition of the Berthelot family, but also and above all the mythi-
cal accomplishment of a lycée student's dream.[23] The whimsical
genealogy that gave him La Fontaine for an ancestor is another
expression of it. Full of disdain for the bourgeois and for the
bourgeoisie, Giraudoux reserved all his respect for the intellectual aristocracy.

The blue blood that was absent from his veins flowed through
his pen. By virtue of that pen, he descended in a straight
line from the purest symbolists, "Mallarmé, Claudel, and Rimbaud,"[24] Romantics without misalliance, "Restif, Chateaubriand,
Chénier, Mme de Staël, Bernardin de Saint-Pierre, Sénancour,
Benjamin Constant, Joubert,"[25] from the great prose writers of
the eighteenth century, "from Diderot and from Rousseau,"[26]
"Diderot, Marivaux, and Chateaubriand,"[27] from scholasticism,
from *marivaudage*, and from *préciosité*,[28] and certainly from
all of the classics, because he was from a generation in which
the rule was "to require the students to lodge in each of their
sentences a conceit, as in Racine, in each paragraph a hyperbole,
as in Mme de Sévigné, and to conclude each assignment with
those heartfelt flourishes which adorn the work of even the
lesser seventeenth-century writers," and because he was of a
time in which "every student conceived his life and his term
papers as poems."[29]

Giraudoux was not content with the nobility of the pen that
went back only to the seventeenth century: "My idea has always
been that the great period of French literature was the period
of the *chansons de geste*. . . . Great poetry is always epic. . . .
The novel in France is precisely what remains of this epic
poetry."[30] Because all true nobility is to be traced back to the
Crusades, here then is our "sweet minstrel" accompanying himself "on the viol."[31] Will he stop there? Not at all: "The language
to which I owe the greatest debt is Latin. You are hearing me
correctly: I do not refer to the Latin of Cicero or Quintillian—the

language of proof and of logical sequence—but to that of those marvelous writers, Pliny, Tacitus, and above all Seneca, whose language is so savory, so full of comparisons, of peculiarities, and in which the component of *improvisation of style* is considerable. Don't forget that I won first prize in the competitive examinations. I could almost say that the first language I ever wrote in a literary way was Latin."[32]

It is hard to believe that these confidential reflections came a quarter of a century after graduating from the lycée. . . .

The second truth: The eternal first did not enter into society through a hidden door, with shoulders bowed and ready to wait his turn in line until his little piece of fame came to him. Without being pushy, for he was, like Simon, "respectful without humility, zealous without zeal," he appeared to his teachers "as the conscience of the class."[33] Whether by merit or by chance, he was, from his second year at the rue d'Ulm, well known to the director, Ernest Lavisse, also the director of the *Revue de Paris* and one of the forty members of the prestigious French Academy.[34] Through personal merit and French charm, during his stay in Munich (July 1905–April 1906), this twenty-three-year-old scholarship recipient struck up friendships in the artistic and aristocratic circles of this capital of the arts.[35] It is true that he owed several of these relationships to a press card from *Le Figaro*, which in the following year would allow him to attend, along with "the emperor, his wife, son, and daughter-in-law," one of the performances given by the Prince of Monaco at the Berlin Opera.[36] At Harvard, the university's illustrious President Eliot, of whom he was to say later, and not without reason, that he was at the time "the moral director of the United States,"[37] took an interest in him that was quite remarkable on the part of the "president of the greatest university in America" for a visiting fellow (October 1907–April 1908). The ambassador of France then introduced him to Theodore Roosevelt, president of the United States, whose hand he shook, and with whom he chatted for several minutes ("questions and answers in French").[38]

All of these relationships were presented in the introduction to a long interview, as follows: "He loved to see celebrities up close: he had himself introduced to William II, to Francis-Joseph, to Roosevelt."[39] *Recollection From Two Existences* gives of his relationships with William II and Theodore Roosevelt a more truthful and also a more humorous account: "The great individuals of the world! If they have touched me, it is only that my life was made up of a series of lithographs for my personal use, for I have not known any of them intimately."[40]

From what follows, however, it would seem that Wilson and even Hitler "made offers" to him, and that he "turned down these offers from giants with flimsy excuses." It appears also that the list of imaginary pictures in which he can be seen in the presence of a sovereign included the regent of Bavaria, Alphonse XIII, and the czar of Bulgaria. Moreover, it began very early, for he had a memory of himself "while still a child in Bessines, at the pharmacy of Monsieur Blondet, being patted on the head by a big man who was travelling across the country in a coach led by mules, who wanted some bicarbonate of soda, and who was the King of Portugal." The mules of the King of Portugal will reappear in scene two of The Paris Impromptu.

This interest in royalty has metaphysical import. The Gardener in Electra explains that "one can conduct on kings experiments that never succeed on paupers."[41] Zelten puts it even better: "For whoever makes a habit of losing his soul, his mediocre soul, the only alibi is to be a king."[42]

Regardless, readers will not be surprised to see Giraudoux conversing with the great individuals of this world, once they have seen Simon the Pathetic serve as secretary to "Bolny, a senator, nearly a millionaire, [who] possessed the most influential newspaper in Europe and who left his country to reign over Paris." "He invited the heads of state one at a time in order to present them to me. . . . So that Georges Duchâtelot, Prime Minister, one day requested me to head his cabinet."[43] Or once they have read the beginning of "Goodbye to War," in Adorable Clio, which leads one to believe (erroneously) that Jean Giraudoux, with pencil and eraser in hand, attended the signing of the Treaty of Versailles on 28 June 1919.[44] Or once they have read the beginning of Bella, or Struggle with the Angel, in which the narrator is the secretary of the Prime Minister. Or when they learn from the newspapers that Edouard Herriot, prime minister in 1932, named Jean Giraudoux to his cabinet, they had the confirmation of what they had been thinking for a long time; that he was the eminence grise of French diplomacy.[45]

What former schoolmates would be surprised to meet him in this way, book after book, in the corridors of power? "I wrote discourses to the Republic as I used to write in our classes— discourses to the prefect and to the bishop, not out of ambition or the desire to be noticed, but simply because I knew how to write better than any of them, and to think with greater precision. . . ."[46]

The third truth: Literature will be the only one particular way of getting to know, on equal terms, the great individuals of this world. For Giraudoux did not enter into literature as others enter into religion. He entered into the history of literature in order to take his place among his peers, aware of what was developing around the *Nouvelle Revue française* in 1909,[47] around the surrealists in 1919, speaking in 1928 in the name of the novelists of his generation,[48] in 1931 in the name of the contemporary theater in France,[49] and, from 1935 on, in the name of France or at the very least of French letters—when it was not in the name of international opinion and men of letters in general.

Literature lives by tradition as much as by innovation. Giraudoux knew this better than anyone: "Plagiarism is the basis for all literature, with the exception of the very first, which is unknown anyway."[50] In other words, "great writers take their material wherever they find it," or still another: "One text can always be concealing another," according to the formula of Gérard Genette in *Palimpsests*.[51] In Giraudoux's case, it must be said: One text always conceals at least another. Indeed, it was not necessary to wait for Genette's book to recognize that *The Odyssey* lies behind *Elpenor*, *Robinson Crusoe* behind *Suzanne and the Pacific*, *The Iliad* between the lines of *Tiger at the Gates*, the Greek tragedies behind *Electra*, La Motte-Fouqué behind *Ondine*, and the Bible behind numerous passages of the novels as well as behind *Judith* and *Sodom and Gomorrah*. Researchers of sources have detected many other reminiscences, allusions, pastiches, parodies, and quotations.[52] The index of *Palimpsests* has the merit of making Giraudoux appear as the champion of "second-degree narrative"—decidedly the eternal first.[53]

Far from hiding that he was crafting a work of literature, he calls the reader to witness, comments on his text in the process of writing it, places a title such as "Draft," or, again, in *Struggle with the Angel*, having written "Chapter Four," begins his chapter as follows:

I am very fond of the first sentences of a chapter which give you by their tone a feeling of total satisfaction about yourself, freeing

you in one second of any apprehension of unanimism, of attachment
to the past, of populism, and clothe the characters for the true
tragedies of the heart—the first sentence of this chapter, for example.* Here it is, rich and drawn from life: . . .

What follows is a sentence of an entire page which one will
reread with a smile, as a pastiche of a fashionable novel.

In *Choice of the Elect*, he has himself photographed in the
process of writing *Choice of the Elect* on the Sunda Islands,
in the course of his trip around the world in the winter of
1938–39:

> That's what was making her return home to Pierre so painful:
> she was expected there by a perfect husband, by a faultless child,
> and by a fatality of the first order. . . . Besides, why should I go
> on today? I am writing these lines off the shores of Timor. On
> an atoll, a completely white Dutchman stands at attention before
> what he believes to be a Dutch ship and which is nothing more
> than a French sentence.[54]

As in the dialogues between the dead with which Simon and
his friends ornamented their assignments,[55] Giraudoux—and
this is one of his secrets as a writer—lived on a footing of
equality among the great individuals, maintained cordial ties
with geniuses, carried every virtue to the point of the superla-
tive: "We thus rated on the highest possible scale—Prometheus
for audacity, Bayard for honor—every man and every feeling."[56]
After this comes a familiar gesture, a bantering word, or an
irreverent thought, which brings us closer to the gods, who
are too distant; to the angels, who are too perfect; and to the
heroes, who are too legendary. These dialogues of the deceased
take place, as is appropriate, in the midst of asphodels and
in the Elysian fields of eternal culture. Placed in a state of
weightlessness in the kingdom outside of time, Giraudoux escapes history, or at least dominates and reconstructs it.** He

---

*Translator's Note: The term unanimism designates a literary school founded
by the writer Jules Romains, who in his youth was a poet in the tradition
of Walt Whitman. Romains' application of unanimism may be seen whimsi-
cally in his play *Knock* wherein a quack doctor cozens an entire village and
profits from its mass hypochondria.

**Translator's Note: The phrase "outside of time" generally conveys the French
word *uchronie*, a term coined by Renouvier, in 1876, for a kind of utopia—an
historical perspective looking back on what might have been possible if history
could be relived.

will not repeat after La Bruyère: "Everything has been said, and we have arrived too late after more than seven thousand years during which men have existed and thought." Rather he would say: "For the billions of years in which there have been worlds and in which there has been life, everything is yet to be said. . . ."*

For "the eternal first" must also be understood in the temporal sense. Just as "the beauty of the world recreates itself every minute,"[57] so too worlds, living beings, and feelings are recreated on each of Giraudoux's pages. With births, rebirths, resurrections, we are always in the first age, on the first day, and his heroes of the first ages hurl themselves forward, in the prime of their youth, from the first hour in the direction of their first love, in the direction of the first love.[58] In his cosmic mythology, the minute of genesis was always begun anew, and he was perfectly aware of it:

The fact is that I still live, like that other, in that internal between creation and original sin. I have been spared the general curse. None of my thoughts is charged with guilt, responsibility, or liberty. Of all of those catastrophes provoked by original sin, the murder of Abel, the Trojan War, the Reformation, and the construction of the Samaritaine department stores, I can wash my hands of them, for I alone in the world have no part in them. By I know not what lineage, I have slipped through the meshes of thousands of generations, not retaining the imprint or the odor of either the Babylonian, the Athenian, or the Carolingian, through the meshes of regret and desire. I see the world's ancient furnishings as Adam saw them, the trees, the ponds, without original sin; and modern inventions, the telephone, the cinema, the automobile, in their divinity. I am a small-scale Messiah for miniscule objects and beasts. I use certain words—including also certain adjectives, my friend—as Adam used them.** I am a small-scale Messiah for three or four expressions. I alone may perceive here and there the being, the insect, the patch of sunlight, which had within its category my happy fate, and was untouched by the curse of God. I am a small-scale Messiah for the patches of sunlight.[59]

---

*Translator's Note: The first citation above is the opening sentence from Jean de La Bruyère's *Les Caractères* (1688). In the sentence that follows, Professor Body is paraphrasing Giraudoux.

**Translator's Note: In the context of the story, the reference to "my friend" is to the schoolmaster who forbade his pupils to use adjectives.

However, birth is very close to death, genesis to the end of
the world, and the first to the last: "It is not only because I
was always first; every class must have its first, as it has its
last. . . ."[60] In the final analysis, the aristocracy of the first rank
unites with the democracy of "everyone in first place":

> *Isabelle.* But there is no first, Mr. Inspector, nor a second, nor
> a third. You surely don't think that I would want to bruise their
> egos. There is the biggest and there is the most talkative, but all
> the little girls are in first place.[61]

The conclusion is provided by the computer, intelligently con-
sulted by Etienne Brunet, a great expert in statistical lexicology:
"It seems that Giraudoux is less concerned with ranking himself
than with distinguishing himself. He loves performance (*exploit,
record, champion* belong to the significant vocabulary) more
than victory . . . and the struggle for first place does not leave
on his face and in his vocabulary the visible trace of effort
(neither *to win [gagner]*, nor *to vanquish [vaincre]*, nor *to beat
[battre]* figure among the significant words). The intensive use
of the word *first [premier]* does not therefore reflect any obses-
sion with classification. Very frequently associated with *time
[fois]*, it expresses the discovery of a world that has changed
and the birth of a new being." The computer thus ranks the
word *first [premier]* alongside other key words: *pure [pur], true
[vrai], perfect [parfait], supreme, pinnacle [faîte], excellence,
height [comble]*, and invites us to discover, with Giraudoux,
"the unique character of each being, of each environment, of
each instant."[62]

Thus the eternal first is a myth. From the viewpoint of literature, it hardly matters that it was a banal blend of biographical
truth and romantic fiction. It matters more that through the
play of distorted information and the distorting imagination,
interferences are created between the author and his characters,
drawing circles within which every reader ends by being included, along with his schoolboy dreams of being either a good
student or the classroom troublemaker. We relive our classroom
days with him. Thanks to the lycée, Giraudoux became not
just a good writer, but the best of companions, and literature
gave him the power to change each reader into a fellow student,
and each fellow student into a unique being, the first of his
type, according to a mechanism of idealization which one must
enjoy and make fun of at the same time: "—We are proud of

you, Simon, you are perfect!"[63] Perfect because the elitism of
Simon is tempered by two "saving graces." Shall one say
"absent-mindedness and laziness," like the Poet in *Ondine?*[64]
One could also call it the sense of equality and gaiety since
not only scholarly hierarchies, but "established regimes, en-
trenched situations, tyrannies, and habits will continue to be
in question as long as there are writers and as long as they
are free with that supreme liberty, which is gaiety."[65]

4

THE PLAYER

Before World War I, Giraudoux would end his day at the café Vachette, which he would not leave until he had played (and won) a bridge game. Between the two wars, he would continue to meet several diplomatic colleagues for interminable nocturnal bridge games, not to mention poker on Sunday with the former Cordeliers. And three months before his death, at the time his mother was dying, according to Maurice Martin du Gard (Vichy, October 1943):

> Jean Giraudoux had not yet seen *Sodom and Gomorrah*, which had opened at the Hébertot Theatre on the 11th; only several scenes, out of sequence, in rehearsal. The day before yesterday, at the Majestic where he regularly played a game of bridge, I brought along Philippe Clément, who had just arrived from Paris, and who, having attended the dress rehearsal, was proud to be able to announce to the author that the play had "worked marvelously. A triumph! And such a distinguished audience!" Giraudoux gave us a handshake that was heavy, warm, feverish. But he was more interested in his game; he was anxious to get back to it.[1]

Thus, right up to the grave, Giraudoux did not stop playing, and not only bridge: athletic games when he was young, and games of chance later on. To imitate Rabelais enumerating the games played by Gargantua, and including only those games that have been documented, Jean Giraudoux played:

at transfers,
at chasing lizards and grasshoppers,
at stirring up vipers and wasps,
at picking up beads from old funeral wreaths in the cemetery,
at swinging on the chains in the fairground,
at climbing on the trapeze with his little girl friends,
at finding birds' nests,

at fishing for crayfish,
at running races,
at bicycle riding,
at swimming, diving,
at soccer,
at rugby,
at being an umpire,
at tennis,
at ping-pong,
at bowls,
at manille,
at pinocle,
at poker,
at bridge. . . .

Let us recall *Bella:*

The French love to play, especially if they are political leaders, and my father knew all the devices by which the generations and the races amuse themselves, all those mild opiates of the people, such as billiards, mah-jong, lotto, and manille. A prime minister cannot withhold his trust from a man who has played bowls with him in the middle of the palace of Madrid. Throughout the evenings of congressional sessions—evenings as deadly as those in a provincial town—my father organized games: dominoes in London, checkers in Spa, spillikins in Cannes. As soon as they got to the dining car, lured to his table by the three-card trick (which, incidentally, he never allowed them to win), presidents would strike up a friendship with him—and it was their own good fortune.[2]

At what did Jean Giraudoux play? To elaborate further. At being an intellectual. At being a practical joker. At being a hopeless lover. At playing a soldier, a leader, and at being in war. At being a diplomat, at being a cabinet attaché, at being the politician. At being a modest man.

I almost forgot: At writing for the theater. "Comic ditty by Mr. Giraudoux, student of the seventh grade" for the "Musical and Literary Evening" of the lycée of Châteauroux.* *The Maiden of Chamignoux*, a play in verse by Jean Giraudoux, unfinished but performed anyway, at Saint-Amand-Montrond, by a group of girls—his cousin and some friends—and with the author,

---

*Translator's Note: The classifications of *sixième* and *cinquième* that appear in this chapter are the rough equivalent of junior high school in the American educational system.

dressed as a girl, starring in the role of the virtuous maiden. *The Voyage of Venus*, by Meilhac and Halévy, at the Ecole Normale Supérieure. *English As It Is Spoken, The Piggy Bank, Esther, Joan of Arc, Godfrey of Bouillon*, if one is to believe the account in *Visitations*: "During my childhood, I spent my days off from boarding school with a large family of cousins and every month we had fun performing on the makeshift stage on Sunday, a play for which an older cousin, who was a Capuchin friar, conducted the rehearsals."[3] Giraudoux does not add that in fact he visited these Toulouse cousins while he was a student in Paris, and that there exists a photograph dated 1907—he was twenty-five and preparing the *agrégation* in German—that depicts him costumed as Mascarille between two female cousins, *précieuses ridicules*.[4] In any event, it is to the Capuchin cousin and to that "happy period of plays called *Miracles*," that we owe the invention of the character of the Archangel, an indispensable dramatic commodity for whoever wishes "to sum up in two sentences everything that has occurred from the creation of the world to the beginning of the play."[5] We have an Angel in *Judith*, an Angel and an Archangel in *Sodom and Gomorrah*; but perhaps there are also some elements of the Archangel ("director of the divine spectacle") in Mercury *(Amphitryon 38)* and in the Beggar of *Electra*, in the Ondine King, in the Gentleman from Bellac, in the Madwoman of Chaillot, and in Paola herself:[6] characters who supervise the staging and who are effective precisely because they do not conceal the fact that they are playacting.*

For Giraudoux made no secret of his playing—except occasionally in a dry-humored way, in order to tease ("no one else teased his friends as often and as amusingly," noted Paul Morand). Let us not make too much of the twenty-three-year-old tutor challenging his fifteen-year-old student to a hundred-meter dash in the heart of Munich; nor even of the junior vice-consul, on his way to a wedding in Allier, who borrowed a handsome uniform and had pinned onto it all the foreign decorations on display in a cabinet in the Department of Protocol.[7] But what of the director of the press department who, scarcely had the journalists departed, was capable of improvising a soccer match

---

*Translator's Note: The French verb *jouer*, like the English infinitive "to play," has the double meaning of play as in games and play as in acting on the stage. The central notion of this chapter is, of course, Giraudoux's proclivity for *playing*, which may best be rendered in English as "playacting."

in the company of his subordinates in his office at the Quai d'Orsay using the office accessories for equipment?[8] What of the famous writer unobtrusively inscribing on a restaurant menu fictitious dishes that the patrons would try to order, beguiled by their price and very alluring names: "illustrated cucumbers, 4,75 F; breast of veal brutally stuffed; houndstooth leg of lamb; and Norway lobster from Elsinore."[9] And what of the Commissioner General of Information who (to an orderly screening those entering the Continental Hotel), instead of showing his pass, identified himself as "Arsène Lupin. This other gentleman is the Count of Monte Cristo, my double."[10]* Even in the office he recommended posting notices such as the following: "In view of the present circumstances, the word *impossible* has again become French."** He often had near him young Merche, a master of the pun. One day when evacuation and withdrawal were being discussed, someone pronounced the word Saint-Pourçain-sur-Sioule. "Saint-Pourçain?" asked Merche. "An eye for an eye!" Then Giraudoux turned to his marshalls: "Gentlemen, do I have a higher bid?"[11]*** And thus even on 7 May 1940, he maintained that: "Neither the frivolous lifestyle nor untrammeled thinking have capitulated under the weight of heavy industry and heavy thinking."[12]

This frivolity has cost him dear. For he gave rein to his taste for puns not only in his light plays like *The Apollo of Bellac*, "laced with capers, verbal acrobatics, and good humor" (in Jouvet's words),[13] but even in his tragedy *Judith*, which was likely to disconcert any believer in the separation of genres. Although during his lifetime he had numerous admirers who believed in his hidden profundity, in his secret gravity, and although the majority of studies devoted to his work present him as an artist (Maurice Bourdet), as a poet (René Lalou), as an engaged writer (Chris Marker), and as a moralist and philosopher (René Marill Albérès),[14] a few harried journalists—who often shape opinion—and Sartre himself, thought Giraudoux

---

*Translator's Note: Arsène Lupin is a detective character—a gentleman burglar who dresses elegantly and wears a mask—who appears in the novels of Maurice Leblanc. The Count of Monte Cristo is the hero of the famous adventure novel by Alexandre Dumas.

**Translator's Note: This is an allusion to the French dictum, "*Impossible* n'est pas français," or "The word *impossible* does not exist in French."

***Translator's Note: The play on words here is that of Saint-Pourçain and "sein pour sein" (breast for breast), which leads to "oeil pour oeil" (an eye for an eye).

was a man of his time, that is to say, an era considered to be as blind as it was fallaciously happy. They relegated him to the era between the wars, condemning him for his frivolity or at the very least refusing to be a party "not only to his game with nature, which is called fantasy, but also to his game with men, which is called poetry."[15]

For writing was for him a game. While writing *Elpenor*, Giraudoux would burst out laughing, the first to be entertained by his own tricks and clever ideas.[16] He shamelessly juggled figures of speech: "No one will criticize my abundance of metaphors when it's obviously a game!"[17] He danced a kind of round in the manner of the Little Eumenides: "—Our specialty is to recite.—What are you reciting? —We do not know in advance. We invent as we go along. But, it is very, very good. . . . Since we come back to the beginning at the end, it is as poetic as it can possibly be."[18] In speaking of his art, it might be useful to recall that he also played the piano, or at least that he tried to, late in life, perhaps too late. At the Ecole Normale Supérieure, he practiced with the awkwardness and obstinacy of a great novice, and his unlucky neighbors—probably students in the school of physics—devised a system of electrical wires that they placed under his piano stool, which burned him badly. Much later, in the small apartment that he rented at 16, rue de Condé in the Odéon district, he had a harpsicord over which his fingers "lightly strayed. He did not play well, but he played with elegance."[19] He went to concerts at the Opera. He had a pleasing baritone voice and he loved to sing. Little by little, however, he channeled into his writing the desire to make himself heard, while maintaining the musicians' privilege which, as Mallarmé has said, is to resist "the very temptation to express oneself." In order to be "musical,"[20] the reticent author did not have to invent any sessions; he had to create a certain harmony, he had to propose a certain interpretation, and he had to bring into play certain techniques that, by their very nature, comprised a certain *game*, as he himself explained it in 1926 to Frédéric Lefèvre:

> It is clear that style is creativity. It is impossible for certain forms in one sentence not to lead to complementary forms in the sentence that follows. A mind reading is like a palm reading. There is an element of *gambling* or of *chance* in each sentence of prose, to the same degree as in verse. . . .

It is this element of improvisation that gives life to a work, and which, above all, gives it poetry.

It is very rare to find any absolute rules in the literary game, and the same goes for playing the piano. . . .

One must be able to play a four-handed arrangement with each of one's characters.[21]

As a bridge player, Giraudoux had perforce to practice combinative analysis. In his theater, the ordering of the scenes and the arrangement of the entrances and exits are governed by a science of the same order.[22] To succeed as a bridge player, he needed not only to see the game unfold in his hand and in the context of the game from his own perspective, but also to imagine it from the point of view of his partner and from the points of view of his opponents. Action and dramatic dialogue are constructed according to the same principle, the responses of one actor fitting those of another as two cogwheels meshing with one another, neither one leaving its own axle or leaving between them any more empty space than is strictly necessary. As a pianist, Giraudoux learned the vital principles of tempo, rhythm, and change of rhythm; of harmony, of counterpoint, of fugue for two, three, or four voices. Is it surprising that he never understood "dramatic architecture as anything other than the articulate sister of musical architecture"?[23]

There is a large difference between this ludic element of writing and the eternal frivolity that has been ascribed to Giraudoux. To deduce, from this frivolity and gaiety, a profound indifference and an "inability to suffer," as Marie-Jeanne Durry and Charles Mauron have done, is the misunderstanding that this reticent writer has made himself vulnerable to.[24] But was he not the author of *School for the Indifferent*? And did not the "pathetic" Simon say: "I do not know how to suffer"?[25]

Giraudoux does know about suffering. He treats the Kitchen Girl with tenderness and his humble characters with sensitivity. Even in the tragedy of Judith, herself a rich girl, is found the following:

In the suburbs of the Lord, on Monday morning, at the hour when nothing exists but the handsome sleeping clerk and the little salesgirl who has spent the night with him for the first time, bending over him and so full of gratitude, anguish and jealousy, so terrified at the prospect of another week in the workshop after her Sunday of sparkling wine and escape, that she kills her lover and then commits suicide.[26]

Another example, in a less passionate but even more pathetic register, is that comic curtain raiser *The Apollo of Bellac:*

> I have an insignificant life, you know. My day is humdrum, and every time I return to my room, I have five flights of stairs to climb in the dark amid the smell of grease. Whether at work or at rest, there is always this prologue of five flights and my loneliness! Sometimes, happily, a cat is waiting in front of a door. I stroke it. A bottle of milk has spilled. I set it upright. If I smell gas, I alert the concierge. Between the third and fourth floors, there is a bend where the stairs are sloped, because of settling and age. At this bend, hope abandons you. At this point, my poor equilibrium hangs in the balance, and my toiling breath is such as those more fortunate have astern their ships. There you have my life! It is made of shadows and of compressed, somewhat bruised flesh. There you have my consciousness: it is a stairwell.[27]

In searching a little and in scraping the shiny polish from the triumphant lycée student and from the powerful diplomat, one discovers at last some secrets, sadly covered over, regarding this other Giraudoux—a very young lycée student, "a child abandoned for eight winters in an icy dormitory": "There could be no mistake: this other person had been unhappy. There was no hiding it from him any more. Each memory which resurfaced from my past contained, too late and to no avail, like the floating bottle of someone shipwrecked, the plea of a child abandoned on a desert island. . . ."[28] Whence came his sympathy for the Stoic philosophy.[29] What secret wounds did he suffer when he fell "from the pinnacle of ten happy years" and made his way down the avenue, which led him from the train station to the lycée, among "the children in tears" whom he described in "Night in Châteauroux"? "During the day, all the poets and all the scientists, and by evening, the solace of the coming night would be needed to comfort a heart so tiny and so empty."[30] Let us refer to the instructions given at the time of his registration in seventh grade (classical studies): "Persons authorized to take him out or visit him in the parlor: nil."[31] Let us imagine what the "melancholy strolls on Thursday" must have been like, in double file under the supervision of the assistant in charge.* Not only on Thursdays and Sundays, but even during certain vacations, little Jean would stay at the boarding school of the lycée. Add to this the social humiliations, evoked indirectly by Simon's father: "Do not get the idea that because you are a scholarship student, you owe nothing to anyone." Nonetheless, he was indebted to the state for that blue ratteen outfit, "the uniform of poverty" thanks to which even today, one may identify on class photographs all the scholarship students. Like Simon: "Thereafter, the child was always dressed in a blue jersey and a pair of black slacks."[32] Simon's father continued: "You are everyone's equal: make your rich friends realize that." But on the occasion of their first communion, the rich students distributed religious pictures printed on the reverse side: "Memento from the first communion of. . . ." One of those pictures bears the name of Jean Giraudoux, not imprinted but written out in the hand of a child attempting to reproduce printed calligraphy. This helps us to understand *Simon* better:

> It was raining and snowing on my past. The child I had believed, until then, to be happy, that I always used to carry joyously on my shoulders, became heavier day by day, making me sink into cold, muddy waters. Perhaps all I would have needed, in order to clear away the cloud, was to see a picture of myself looking carefree and joyous. But I had no photographs of my childhood. My father did not hold with photographers, any more than he did with dentists and eye doctors. They had economized on my teeth, on my eyes, and on my photographs.[33]

It is difficult to verify this statement with respect to the dentists and the eye doctors, but with respect to photographers it is certainly true: the pictures we have of Jean Giraudoux as a child and as an adolescent are all group photographs taken with family or schoolmates.

Let us not read too much into these sad memories, and let us not abuse autobiographical interpretation. In writing the story of *Simon*, separated from his mother, as is the case in certain pages of *Provincial Ways*, Giraudoux borrowed as much from his reading as from his own life and re-edited, in a certain manner, the books that he had adored, like *Redhead* and *The*

---

*Translator's Note: Thursday afternoon was the mid-week break from classes in the French educational system.

*Little Fellow.** The *Little Fellow*, in fact, might provide us with something like a point of reference. The episode reported by his classmate Aucuy is widely known: "One day, in the seventh grade, during the evening study session, Giraudoux was reading avidly . . . a collection of serial episodes carefully cut out of newspapers and bound by hand. When the vice principal, Duchâteau, expressed surprise, he replied, 'My mother gave it to me to read.' After which Duchâteau relaxed and said simply: 'I am somewhat surprised that your mother recommended this reading to you. But I appreciate her exceptional wisdom!'"[34]

Why would this mother, knowing that her son was abandoned for months on end to the tenderness of the school administrators, have had him read *The Little Fellow*? To apologize? To place the burden of guilt on the father? To empathize with her son? And why did the vice principal, this illustrious Gédéon Duchâteau, who seemed to incarnate all the tenderness with which Giraudoux endowed the civil servants in his works—isn't that right, Commissioner?—why did Duchâteau, after being surprised at such reading material, defer to the "exceptional wisdom" of Giraudoux's mother?** Is it necessary to blame all the misfortunes of the child on a father who was too strict and too miserly or who earned too little to satisfy the tastes and ambitions of his wife and his son, who for their part could only endure and communicate silently? In Giraudoux's family, both immediate and extended, this interpretation is disputed; the memory of the father, a kind man if ever there was one, is defended. Neither the biographical details, when we have them, nor Giraudoux's subsequent work encourage further research in this direction, were it not for the desire to turn every man, at all costs, into a new Oedipus.

In any event, one could find other scars poorly healed, other smarting memories. For example, wounded birds, birds that have had their eyes poked out, blind birds, birds which have been strangled, dead birds. Will psychoanalytical criticism one day be mired in this area? Giraudoux's work is so rich that

---

*Translator's Note: These two children's books, *Poil de Carotte* (Redhead) by Jules Renard (1864–1910) and *Le Petit Chose* (The Little Fellow) by Alphonse Daudet (1840–97), are household words in France. The two books relate stories of difficult and unhappy childhoods, much like Dickens's *David Copperfield*.

**Translator's Note: The reference to the Commissioner (Le Contrôleur) is the modest civil servant character who appears at the end of the novel *Suzanne and the Pacific*, and who becomes a major character in the play *Intermezzo*.

it would offer ten other approaches that are as fertile and adventuresome. Why treat like a deranged person a man who, throughout his life, projected the image of a superior human being, of a successful life and work? And why judge him incapable of performing the primary analysis of himself?

Two things are certain: the experience of suffering and the will to overcome it. "I do not know how to suffer," said Simon, but he continued: "Instead of suffering, I waited. I waited for I know not what response; I was waiting for the door to open. I wandered in the streets, looking behind me whenever I heard footsteps."[35] To fight against suffering, he summoned up an invincible hope; against the egotism of suffering, the generosity of pity; against the weight of the past, the incentive of a future to be forged; against the cult of suffering of a decadent literature, the call to a philosophy of the waking dream, which later will be called the "messianism" of Giraudoux.[36] A sensitive and precocious child, pushed a bit early out of the familial nest, he devised a defense system, a little like that described by Geneviève in the early versions of *Siegfried*: "You must realize that at my age I have a formula for raising the painful areas of my thoughts one notch—ten notches—on the scale of insensitivity. Even with a minimum of resignation, a maximum of automatism is all that is required for an intelligent being to succeed in suffering no more pain in life than that of the corns on one's feet."[37]

A minimum of resignation, a maximum of automatism. Thus was Giraudoux's own heart regulated, better than any alarm clock: full of hope and looking toward the future, but also protected by gilt paper against the disappointments and the buffeting of life. He was at the same time sensitive to everything pathetic and methodically indifferent. On the one hand, he was able to say, like Simon: "I came to know intimately those who didn't have great opportunities, or great hopes, and who have accommodated themselves to life as one does on an island." And on the other hand, to proclaim, again like Simon: "My suffering? I had exchanged the heart where it dwells for a well-lit, resonant house."[38] He cultivated schizophrenia, to which every psyche is prone, and practiced a methodical splitting of all his senses, attentive to every echo, every reflection, every image of himself. From an unpublished page of a notebook: "He had invented a camera to photograph himself: the narcissus." Simon went even further: "My refuge was the mirror over the fireplace; I would rest my elbows in front of it, cooling

my brow on it; I would see my reflection leaning towards me. . . .
For a long time, I had no other consolation than to see, near
or far, this poor double playing my role and suffering for me."[39]

"Playing my role"—in using the double, Giraudoux was escap-
ing suffering through playacting and through theater. Those who
knew him describe his courtesy as a kind of coldness, his affabil-
ity as a façade. Did he not describe himself under the name
of *Jacques the Egotist?* He was egotistical, in the frank opinion
of a few, and only a very small number of people were truly
dear to him: his mother, his son, most definitely; a handful
of friends, perhaps. Beyond this limited circle, he was a good
friend and a congenial colleague, and he also recognized family
ties. But here we are already dealing with the social "scene,"
that is, the social "game"—that is, playacting. His success in
the theater could be explained by an old routine of role playing,
or actually playing more than one role. As his correspondence
and various witnesses attest, he did not speak the same language
and was not the same man to everyone. And so it is possible
to recognize him in several characters in the same play. He
obviously empathizes with Siegfried, but so does he also with
Zelten. In *Tiger at the Gates,* one hesitates to hazard a guess
as to who is the author's spokesman: the Geometrician is a
grotesque crybaby who comes to present arguments to the
wretched clan of bellicose old men, but his monologue on "the
footsteps of Helen, the elbow of Helen, the range of her glance
and of the voice of Helen" is pure Giraudoux, a Giraudoux
of whom he is making fun.[40]

Thus Giraudoux creates his double and observes himself, but
it is the converse of Narcissus. He is not the creature of suffering
flesh hunched over his brilliant reflection; he *is* that reflection,
immaterial, moved only by the rippling of the water: "A chasm
separated me from my life; I remained alone on the other side."[41]
Not content with living "in this interval which separated Creation and original sin,"[42] he dreamed of the period which preceded Creation, of the time when the atoms which make up
the human heart were still floating, separated and indistinct
in space: "How much lighter we are with these billions of tiny
hearts than with a single heart! At long last, we were weightless,
without chains . . . except for this weight on the chest cavity,
no doubt where the empty space used to be."[43]

Like Jerome Bardini, he has a feeling of "nausea at the idea
of Creation,"[44] this sort of chemical precipitation which upset
the purity of ether and brought forth the law of gravity, weight,

and the fermentation of matter. "He accepted human pressure on himself only to the degree in which it resembled the pressure of air."[45] He wanted to be Ariel. Thus it would be vain to submit his work to traditional psychological commentaries. Giraudoux takes a stand exactly opposite to the Socratic dictum "know thyself," and he intends, like Simon, to spare himself "the vile task of knowing himself";[46] like Nausicaa, dreaming of "a total stranger."[47] Each being, each object presented itself as a secret to be kept.

The word *secret* serves as a bond among numerous heroes of Giraudoux. Don Manuel the Lazy: "The secret is no longer at the heart of our love, to sustain it, like the seed in the fruit."[48] The Prince in *End of Siegfried*: "It seems to me that for some time now secrets have been tiring very quickly of their function of being secrets."[49] Rémy Grand in "The Mirage of Bessines": "We have to behave towards our own thought with greater prudence and secrecy than towards people who are different and hostile."[50] The Commissioner of *Intermezzo*: "I'm not in favor of understanding secrets. An unexplained secret often occupies in you a place that is more noble and more airy than its explanation. It's like the air bubble in a fish."[51] And even Helen of Troy: "I don't really like getting to know others' feelings. . . . I don't really like getting to know my own feelings, either."[52]

Psychoanalysts have a word for this need for secrets, this refusal to know oneself: the word *repression*. What this word means is a feeling of terror when confronted with the depths of the unconscious, flight from one's own nature, naive projection onto daily life. Charles Mauron tosses Jung's formula at Giraudoux: "If you do not want to know your *anima*, you will meet up with her again one day, and you will marry her." And in his analysis: "Thus, Giraudoux's heroes often marry a universe that is only the projection of their innermost souls. In a crisis, they think they are consulting the stars, the trees, and the furniture when in fact they are only consulting their own subconscious."[53] And indeed, woe betide anyone who pronounces the name of Freud in Giraudoux's presence! One should reread "The Mirage of Bessines" and the story of Rémy Grand, the story of a false psychosis that will be instantly liquidated by a pilgrimage to the sources of childhood:

As for all those adulterous or incestuous attachments to our wet nurses or to our first cousins once removed, by which psychology now explains the very fabric of our sensibility, Rémy felt that his own affair with the flora and fauna of Bessines had not been touched by any of it. . . . Then Rémy stood upon the hilltop. . . . He cried out insults at the top of his lungs that were repeated by his echo: "—Shit on you," he shouted! "And tough shit for psychology, and physiology, and psychophysiology. And shit on Sigmund Freud."[54]

Let me cut short the quotation here, for if I do not, the same swear word will ring out three more times, even though Giraudoux hardly ever used it in his writing and could boast that "his speech was free of slang, his thoughts free of hatred," with the above exception.[55] One might even say it is not an exception when it is a question of Freud or of Freudianism, which he never spares. Whether it be in *Intermezzo*: "Superstition . . . Freudianism."[56] Or in his *Gérard de Nerval*: "How much better off we'd be, in our time, if the word Freudianism came not from Freud, but from *Freude!*"[57] Or in *The Five Temptations of La Fontaine*: "La Fontaine had the good luck to live in a period when the psychiatrists had not turned the subconscious into a person immensely more rational and clear-thinking than consciousness itself."[58]

Giraudoux's nervous system was badly shaken by the war. Transferred to the hospital of Fougères after the Battle of the Marne, he suffered from insomnia and from nightmares: "For me, the Prussians continued bombing Fougères at night as they bombed my trench."[59] After the war, and as he was turning forty, he went through one of those "life crises" that he has described so well, not without confronting the "neurasthenic demon."[60] "He had believed he was haunted and damned: but he himself soon had to acknowledge that everything in him was healthy and rational."[61] The Freudian theories, which his young surrealist friends were promoting, might have interested him. Had he not always been alert to the subconscious? Did he not practice automatic writing as a sort of liberation from inner drives? Did he not make a point of retelling his dreams, and had he not responded to a survey: "The dream of my life? To recall my dreams"?[62] Charles Mauron goes so far as to suggest that Giraudoux "borrows from psychoanalysis not only explanations . . . but actually a method of investigation."[63] And yet, Giraudoux was possibly describing himself under the name of Gilbertain when he said: "He was the negation of Freud and of all modern literature."[64] (By "modern literature," here is meant all literature with a pretention to the psychological.)

In chapter five of *Juliette in the Land of Men*, Giraudoux wrote a savage satire of the type of novelist who "followed you everywhere without understanding anything—that is to say, a true psychologist."[65] The entire art of the novelist Lemançon, a specialist in language and in the feminine soul, consists in covering the universe "with a verbal crust which hid the chasms of chaos from him" and his latest invention, the "Interior Monologue," resembles the "utterances of old men talking to themselves." From her visit to the man of letters "all dripping with stream-of-consciousness, a visit "which ended in the defeat of psychology, of psychophysiology, and in the death of style," Juliette retained the lesson that "any human being who doesn't know how to turn a deaf ear, is a trapdoor by means of which evil inundates the world," and that the interior monologue is the opposite of "Interior Silence."[66]

To bend an ear toward the somatic depths to hear nothing but libidinous stories, to probe into childhood only to confine it into the possessive and castrating circle of the bourgeois family, to analyze dreams and meet only the decadent phantasms of the Austro-Hungarian Empire? Giraudoux takes Freudian theories to task explicitly for besmirching the image of childhood,[67] disseminating impurity and "bluffing" the naive (he uses this expression in *Five Temptations*),[68] and also for dwelling on the past and closing the human monad in upon itself. The therapy he prescribes, on the other hand, consists in keeping quiet, in imitating animals[69] and plants,[70] and in putting oneself in touch with the universe.[71]

After her visit to Lemançon, Juliette comes to see him as well, Jean Giraudoux, the author-character. And Jean Giraudoux, instead of letting his heart and mind empty themselves "like a broken hour glass," reads to Juliette a text that he has just written, since that is his function as a writer and a poet, a "sluice gate of language." This text is the "Prayer on the Eiffel Tower," a text resolutely modern, futuristic, and revolutionary, and which thus takes the "Prayer on the Acropolis," Renan, and Renan's rationality a step further, raising them to the heights of Paris (the new Athens) and of the Eiffel Tower (the new Acropolis), thence to contemplate "the five thousand square miles of the world where the most thinking, the most talking, and the most writing have taken place"; "to link names one to another by direct electrical current" in order to continue "the battle against ugliness, tyranny, and matter," to let people breathe "this heady air, this spaciousness"—"the accumulated stratifications of the mind, of reason, of taste."[72]

Appearing in his novel as a writer, Giraudoux does not want the persona of the writer to be substituted for the function of the writer and become an obstacle to it. Giraudoux the man is nothing but a marvelous writing and thinking machine. Giraudoux the man is nothing so that the writer can be everything. Here he reaches the extreme of secretiveness, which consists in making others believe, like Jacques the Egotist, that he has no secrets. Jean Giraudoux invites us to treat him as he treated Racine and Nerval—without biographical considerations. Let it be said that Nerval remained a man of letters until his death, and that "at the extreme and diabolical point of his personal life, he observed the conventions and the joys of his profession."[73] Let it be known that the adolescence of Racine "was no less theoretical" than his childhood; that "he did not think of his own death when the word death came to his pen, any more than he did about his shadow when he wrote the word shadow, or about the woman he loved when the word lover came to him"; that "there was in him no feeling which was not a literary feeling," and that "the most profound discoveries of the human heart were made from an infinite distance from himself, through deduction, on souls long vanished and sometimes invented, like the ones of Andromache or Phaedra, just as the true laws of our planet have been discovered from stars that have burnt out or are barely visible."[74]

Hence two themes recurring throughout his work emerge, both often studied and, moreover, closely tied to one another: the idea of physical and moral purity, of transparence, or cleanliness (of body and of language), themes tied to symbols drawn from water and air; and the themes of depersonalization, of anonymity, of amnesia—diametrically opposed to psychoanalysis, the negation of all *psyche*. Jean Giraudoux presents himself as Siegfried, as Jerome Bardini, with the "ideal sports jacket": "His pockets were not bulging; . . . one guessed that he carried neither wallet nor identity papers, nor even letters."[75] The Ulysses of *Elpenor* is not content, as was Homer's, with pretending that he was called Nobody (and even "the son of of Nobody, the grandson of of of Nobody").* He persuades the Cyclops that he is no more than an appearance, an image conceived in the

---

*Translator's Note: Giraudoux frequently enjoys taking liberties with syntax and language, as in this playful use of multiple prepositions.

mind—even though he proves to him shortly after, and cruelly, that it is hardly likely that "the imaginings of a boor could be Greeks, and that a Cyclops's brain could invent the idea of Ulysses without bursting."[76] To the ridiculous claim to be someone—which is in fact a "terrible anonymity"[77]—he opposes all the games of abstraction, of thought, and of culture, thanks to which the writer rediscovers not only his power as a magician and as an illusionist, but his capacity to shape reality. The poetics of metamorphosis lead finally to a political system for the imagination. For, as Giraudoux explains in a preface to a manual on playing bridge: "Houses made of cards have proven to be far more solid, of late, than towns and citadels."[78] The ruse of Ulysses, alias Nobody, alias Giraudoux, is to have understood, by dint of contingent behavior and algebraic combinations, that the distinguishing feature of any game, as of writing, of playthings, and of the theater, "is to be real within the unreal."[79]

5

FEMININE SINGULAR

"When I see her, my heart is so full that I feel it might burst."[1] Who is "she"? She is legion—she is *all* women. Each one special in her own way, multiplied into millions of models. All different, yet all of the opposite sex, on the opposite side—for all eternity. . . .

His mother, first of all, was unique. Anne Lacoste, who was called Antoinette, and after her marriage, Antoinette Giraudoux, mother of the writer, was tall, beautiful, intelligent, "and very wise," according to the vice principal, Gédéon Duchâteau. The daughter of a veterinarian, she was, on the ladder of social advancement, one generation ahead of the kind man she married, the son of a peasant.[2] In fact, the Giraudoux side of the family was virtually ignored, and the family reunions brought together only the Lacoste side of the family.

The mother stayed at home to raise her children, while the father was off on his trips as a tax collector or double-checking his figures. A frail mother after bringing her boys into the world, a sickly mother when her sons left her, so that "Mama's health" occupied ten times more space in her son's letters than did the activities of the father.[3] She was a mother who was a slave to tradition, who stood and served her menfolk seated at table.[4]

In return, when her boys were students, they came home to see her at every possible occasion. Later on, the older son settled in his medical practice close to her, and the younger would come back frequently to see her: as a diplomat at Christmas, Easter, and in the summer; as a soldier for a day, for a few hours, with or without leave, abandoning his sweetheart, his girl friends, and his wife. The father died in 1921. The mother, for all her fragile health, would live to be ninety-one, and her son Jean would barely outlive her: it is said that he caught cold at her funeral. Unable to recover from the grippe, he survived her by less than three months.[5]

Let us begin, then, with the mother. From his mother came the love of books, the literary sensibility, the refinement. Hence the following paradox: while Giraudoux readily projected onto the screen of his imagination an affectionate caricature of a frugal and authoritarian father (the little bureaucrat with principles[6] who, let it be said for the record, was not like his father at all, or, only very little[7]), he never spoke of his mother in his books, except to imagine in *Simon the Pathetic* that she had died while bringing him into the world.[8] Absent from the stories themselves, the mother is in a sense omnipresent in his work, which was written with all the heritage of her blood, written possibly out of competition for her with his older brother, for whom she obviously had a preference, and written to repay her caresses and to cry out for more:

> Man always needs caressing and loving.
> His mother showers him with love the moment he sees
> the light of day,

sing the indolent natives of *Supplement to Cook's Voyage,* following the words of Alfred de Vigny.[9]

The verb *caress* is used by Giraudoux at every opportunity and for every conceivable subject: "All that I ask today is that I be given for my fatherland a country that I can at least caress," says Siegfried-Forestier.[10] The war stories grouped under the title *Adorable Clio* bear on the title page the epigraph: "Forgive me, o war, for having caressed you at every opportunity I could find. . . ." Was this a quest for an epidermal happiness, only skin-deep? Rather, it was a quest for the critical point where the flesh joins the nervous system and where the surface reveals the essence: "I find enough depth in the surface of the world."[11] In this sense, he can also say: "I am the poet who most closely resembles a painter"[12]—but also the writer who most closely resembles a lover.

Between the mother and the lover, there was the verdant paradise of youthful love;[13] there were childhood sweethearts;[14] and there were sweet female cousins. Let us recall Agnes: "I have a cousin who's not bad-looking: I'm going to practice on him."[15] Jean Giraudoux often spent his vacations in Saint-Amand-Montrond with his first cousins, Renée Lacoste (two or three years his elder) and Jeanne Lacoste, in whose honor he entitled

Jean and Jeanne, a handwritten, illustrated newspaper, "Editor: Jean Giraudoux." At this time, in fact, Jean could scarcely have been more than eleven years old, and Jeanne was still in her crib, for they were eleven years apart. But then they grew up, and Jeanne, according to the account of her older sister, "became a charming and distinguished young lady, for whom he had a brotherly affection"[16]—the baby sister, that is, that his parents never gave him. But this is exactly the case of the little sick boy of *Provincial Ways.*[17] "From my window," dreaming of a sister he does not have:

> When I open my eyes, I see my sister—my sister whose name I shall never reveal to you. And when I close my eyes, images pass by which resemble her. . . . Then, the lamp; the lamp is lighted. . . ; the wooden floor glows like the ocean depths; a gentle shadow plays over them weightlessly, in order to bring to me—o, my sister— your fair hair through which I run my fingers. . . .[18]

Perhaps he played Cherubino with his aunt's linen maids.[19] In any event, one can hardly confuse the author of *Provincial Ways* with that character who mentions, in the short list of his degrading memories, a visit to a tiny street of ill repute, and who therein "one night became a man all at once, at around the time of [his] *baccalauréat.*"[20]

The young lycée graduate, moving to Paris, met up with a host of male and female cousins of all ages, with whom he put on plays on Sunday afternoons. In this Toulouse family who, as though by predestination, lived on the rue du Théâtre in the Grenelle district, the mother had passed away, and the older sister exemplified every virtue. She was so pious that she eventually took her vows as a Carmelite nun, and she died in 1913. Jean was seen weeping at her funeral.[21] He was certainly thinking of her when he wrote "Until Bethany," the scenario for *Angels of Sin,* for the heroine, upon entering the convent, obtains permission to keep in her religious life the first name she had had in the world: Anne-Marie. A younger sister of Anne-Marie, Amélie, had died in 1908. Jean Giraudoux had visited her before leaving for America, when the doctors had declared her case hopeless.[22] That visit is like the one described in *School for the Indifferent,* when Don Manuel the Lazy appears at the bedside of his young cousin, Renée-Amélie, as she is dying.[23]

Thus, like an overgrown adolescent, Jean Giraudoux prized

family intimacy and postponed the time for romantic love: "I am afraid of everything that is *new*, as if that which preceded it might die; I am afraid of all *beginnings*, as of a commitment."[24] When, after twelve years of dormitories and barracks, Giraudoux the student left for Germany on a scholarship, he would learn to make the most of his freedom, and thereby protect it. In Munich, as in Sassnitz, "we were a band of young people (by young people I also mean young women), and familiarity with the Germans progressed at a fast pace."[25] Was there in Munich a certain Martha, too loving and too beloved, as he related in *Siegfried and the Limousin?*[26] Certainly in Berlin, in a few days, he made the conquest of the maid at the Rosen boardinghouse, Lisel, who pursued him with passionate letters.[27]

His stay at Harvard University remains forever emblazoned with American coeds, and *La Grande Revue* was correct in billing "Don Manuel the Lazy" as a study of flirtation in the United States: "I truly feel that this nation is the land of young girls."[28] He could have said like Simon: "Young girls alone interested me."[29]

Paris was no less the land of young girls. In the ancient convent of the Cordeliers[30] where Engène Morand, director of the School of Decorative Arts,[31] had the use of an apartment, every Sunday a small band congregated, which was destined to be inseparable: Paul, the son of the household, whom Jean Giraudoux had tutored in Munich in the summer of 1905; Jean Giraudoux, who had become a second son in this hospitable home; Suzanne Lalique, the daughter of the famous glassmaker and ten years younger than Jean, who was like an adopted child of the Morands; Denise Rémon, whose father said to Jean Giraudoux: "Here, read this" ("this" was *Swann's Way*, which had just appeared in print); and one of the cousins of the Morands, Eirik Labonne, a future French governor in Morocco. After the death of the Morand parents and the marriage of the members of the little band—Suzanne Lalique to Paul Haviland, a son of the American family that had become porcelain makers in Limoges; and Denise Rémon to Edouard Bourdet, administrator of the Comédie française in 1936—the Sunday reunions continued, marked by the ritual card game that would be immortalized in a photograph.[32] Though fickle in love, Jean Giraudoux would be more than faithful in friendship: in fact, uncompromising when it came to faithfulness, blaming those who were absent, and himself neglecting all other ties. In Suzanne Lalique, he had the little sister that he had dreamed of for such a long time—as pretty as the pictures she painted.[33] And he told Denise that she, Denise, was pretty too.

Thus, casual romances and tender friendships prolonged his adolescence. Were his ties with a Mrs. Adams any closer? Her husband wanted to bring him into his business, but Jean Giraudoux kept his distance from him as well as from her. Judging from the account of their crossing the Atlantic from America to Europe, in *Provincial Ways*,[34] and also from the dialogue between Don Manuel and Mrs. California Asterell, who was modeled on her,[35] it seems that in this case too he preferred flirtation and friendship to love:[36] "I move towards her. . . . I'm in no hurry. Happiness is no burden on the condition that you take it easy—like hauling a boat. And for the brief time I have left to be a child, I want one last chance to revel in the world's childish activities."[37]

The God of love, when one escapes his clutches for a long time, has all the more leisure to fill his quiver, and arrows that have been sharpened at length are all the sharper for it. Giraudoux spent the first part of his life subject to the rules of the lycée, the boarding school, the barracks, and war, which at that time meant living in a world without women. "Most of the time that I could have spent with women in my youth, I devoted to men of genius. It was with them that I had my first dates and my first heartbreaks."[38] The lovers of his youth were called Eurydice, Cleopatra, Thais; his teachers of the art of loving were Lamartine, Hugo, Vigny, and Ovid.[39] Culture and literature swelled the sails of the imagination. And how they did! What splendid loves he, too, used to dream about. During at least ten years of abstinence, the caresses of the writer-lover were generated by meditations on mystical love, from the androgyne of Plato's hermaphrodite to the *Dialogues on Love* by Léon Hebreu, and by everything that the troubadors, the cabalists, the precious writers, the illuminists, and the French and German Romantics had been able to crystallize in precious gems and translucent stones around the mere name of Woman.[40] Whence a twofold quest that runs throughout his life and his work: one, which is mystical, of the ideal woman, and the other, which is poetic, of women whose sensibility is independent of the deceitful circle of idealization and culture. On the one hand, the account in *Simon*: "I was looking for my fiancée. . . . Why couldn't I have my superplanetary woman, my Uranian woman? . . . It was almost the grace of God; it was tenderness. . . . If love consists in loving *everything*, then I am already in love!'[41]

On the other hand, the testimony from *Adorable Clio:* "I write before women as if before a model; not a word which I wrote at more than five meters from them."[42]

This confrontation between the ideal woman and those observed in the flesh does not result in the usual trite conclusion: disillusionment, the revilement of reality—something like Proust's kiss of Albertine, wherein desire is quenched in satisfaction-dissatisfaction. On the contrary, the real woman is more beautiful than the woman of his dreams:

> The word beauty does not suffice, nor the word youth, nor the word perfection. . . . I reproached myself, as for a mean and feeble act, for not having imagined so much beauty, such brilliance, and often in our first meetings, upon seeing her, I felt fading from my heart an Anne humbler and diminished in size, and who for a long time would return in the evenings to live in mediocrity in her dazzling place.[43]

It would be a mistake to take this for a hyperbolic gallantry. In the world of Giraudoux's imagination, reality and preciosity merge. Driven by "confidence in happiness" as much as by "desire for reality," Giraudoux for his readers, like Eglantine for her lovers, "transposed into reality the nerves and the senses of dreams."[44]

How many women posed before the poet-painter, the writer-lover? It is difficult to say. First, one must make a distinction between sweethearts and Love itself. But how does one sort them out? "It was springtime, the brother of summer. You could not have told the wheat from the grass, nor friendship from love." What portrait of a woman, in the works of Giraudoux, could not have been given the title of the third of the "Allegories" in *Provincial Ways,* "To Friendship, to Love"?

> The pond had no reflections, the sun no shade, the windows no sunlight. Friendship or Love, I took her hand. . . .
> If happiness is having lips which are about to laugh, eyes which are about to cry, and an enormous hat with a dozen feathers, then no one may brag about being happier than my girlfriend. . . . Friendship is no more, love is no more; there is nothing else on your dress and on your face than a shimmering and a radiance from which your whole being trembles, and which forces me to move anxiously towards you, while you lean over the edge of the rowboat looking at your own reflection.[45]

It is thus impossible to make the distinction and difficult
to ascertain: "On the subject of women, the two of us were
modest and discreet," relates Paul Morand. Now Paul Morand,
who was the greatest "consumer of women" of his generation,[46]
if not the most inconstant husband in history, told me, in the
indiscreet though polished words of a veteran diplomat, speaking of his friend Giraudoux: "He served ladies very well." How
did he know? Through a common mistress? Never will one
find such a remark from Giraudoux's pen, at least without metaphor; in other words, without transposition; in other words,
without transports.[47] The kind of love that would not produce
transports, that would produce only pleasure, would be neither
love nor friendship. It would be better to protect oneself from
it with a blow of the sword; thus Judith prefers the death of
her lover to the death of love. Again, it is difficult to make
a distinction and difficult to define: "It is somewhere, don't
you think, between crucifixion and hysterical laughter, hives
and death?"[48]

Love is not synonymous with marriage. But love itself cannot
exist without social implications, above all during a period when
a woman's status could be determined by her dress, and even
more unmistakably by her class:

> "Is she a princess, that she dares to present herself like that? . . ."
> "No, she's rolling in dough. Can't you feel it, surrounding that
> simplicity: fancy cars and jewels with safety clasps? I'm sure that
> when she goes out of the house, she hasn't even touched her dress
> or her hair. She's one of those who never has to prepare herself
> for either love or death—she's a rich girl, that's all!"[49]

Elegance, distinction, and finery are reserved to a few select
women, who fascinated Giraudoux all the more since he was
rich only in pride and unrestrained ambition: not the ambition
of a fortune hunter, nor of an upstart, but rather that of a seeker
of absolutes. To be a god for her, to appear like Apollo, and
strike like a thunderbolt—Oh! The brightness of that first look
at you, O Stephy, O Judith, Tessa, and you, Ondine—and that
she then become a queen, if not a goddess, desired before she
has been introduced, and loved before she has been seen.

Simon was already smitten, not only with the desire to make
the acquaintance of Anne, but with Anne herself, without having
seen her, and simply, quite simply, because she was promised
to him by Helen—Helen, the friend that Gabrielle had concealed

from him; Gabrielle, the niece of Madame de Liville.[50] A similar network of conspirators had been necessary so that the son of the tax collector of Cusset should be introduced to Madame Grancher, the heiress of huge plantations and the widow of Professor Grancher of the Faculty of Medicine in Paris, who was destined for immortality thanks to the Grancher Foundation; so that Madame Grancher should point out to her nephew the presence of Jean Giraudoux at Harvard University in 1907–8; so that this nephew should happen to be the oldest son of one of the wealthiest families in Cuba, which owned in particular half of the city of Havana; and so that Pierre Abreu, this enormously wealthy heir, should send an invitation to Jean Giraudoux during his stay at Harvard. Here is the story as related in a letter sent to Cusset:

> Madame Grancher's nephew resides in a luxurious apartment in one of the enormous dormitories for rich students. I smoked in his quarters some excellent Havana cigarettes, imported directly, and I regret not having accepted a magnificent cigar that I would have enclosed with my letter to be used by the tax collector. He showed me some photographs of their house, which is a palace, while inviting me to take advantage of it, as well as a photo of a young chimpanzee which his mother takes with her everywhere and which is going with her to New York, Egypt, and Europe.[51]

The travels of the chimpanzee are proof that, at a certain level, wealth is no longer a matter of money, but is actually closer to the Latin sense of the word *fortune*: the possibility of arranging one's own destiny, the right to all eccentricities, absolute freedom. At the time, Jean Giraudoux was unable to purchase a coat or go to the dentist, for it was too expensive, and he tabulated his expenditures each evening.[52] A plague on bookkeeping and finances! We have landed squarely in the domain of metaphysics and in the world of the novel.

Jean did not write this to his father, but Pierre Abreu had also shown him the photograph of his sister, and told him her name: Lilita. Two years later, Lilita arrived in Paris and resided on the rue Beaujon, in her aunt's house. At the time, Jean Giraudoux was taking his meals on credit at the Laveur, the restaurant for impoverished students. Having quit one and then two part-time jobs in order to devote himself to preparing for the consulate examinations, he had learned with dismay the preceding month that the pupil to whom he was giving private lessons

was suddenly leaving for three weeks in Portugal.[53] A prisoner
in his own dwelling, like one of his heroes, on "the days when
there was nothing in the kitty and he had to complete some
menial task in order to stay alive,"[54] he placed several short
stories in the *Matin* and, was, according to several sources,
a tour guide at the Louvre. He lived "from one day to the next,"
as he wrote to his parents.[55]

Lilita was going to be twenty in the fall—eight years younger
than Jean. She was a beautiful brunette, passionate, and a lover
of culture. Jean was her tour guide—this time without pay—one
afternoon each week, around the monuments and the various
districts of Paris. (Meanwhile, Jean was toying with phantasma-
gorical projects of "colossal" fortunes in the mines of Peru and
Chile, the construction of a 3,000-kilometer railway, and a contract paying him $6 million . . . in shares in a company that
had yet to be created.[56]

Jean wrote to Lilita every week to confirm the date of their
next excursion through Paris, and Lilita kept all of his letters.[57]
Jean's financial situation eased after he became junior vice-
consul, attached to the political and commercial department
of the Minister of Foreign Affairs; but it remained at a very
modest level. Not so long ago junior vice-consuls received no
salary, but Giraudoux was paid—"in a monthly stipend, if not
in gold coins."[58] His salary was on a par with the student scholarship that he received in Munich from 1905–6![59] His debts to
the Laveur were not settled until 1917; still, he could never
resist the temptation to purchase sketches by Poussin, using
the system that he would later describe in *Siegfried and the
Limousin*: "In exchange for some money that I handed over,
not in payment for them, but in payment of previous debts."[60]
As for Lilita, she spent the fall at Cambo-les-Bains, then left
to spend six months in America. She spent the summer in
Brittany, so that one and a half years after their first meeting,
Jean still addressed her ceremoniously as "Mademoiselle" and
closed his letters with the assurance of his "respect" and
"devotion"—accompanied by greetings to Madame Grancher.
But this politeness in writing (only slightly enlivened with witti-
cisms and greatly encumbered with gongorisms) must have co-
existed with a certain amount of taunting in the course of their
meetings—taunts that Lilita interpreted as ridicule and were
undoubtedly no more than the teasing games by which prolonged adolescence protects itself. Finally, when Lilita turned
twenty-one, Jean Giraudoux, now the author of two books, grew

bolder and the forty-sixth letter of 13 February 1912, ends with "I love you." The letters that follow shed light on the two years that had just flown by:

> Tomorrow will mark two years since our walk in Montmartre. You told me as you were leaving me, and already becoming ill: "I liked you more today than the other times. . . . Your tone wasn't quite so mocking. . . ." I've lived with those words for six months.[61]

And as if these four lines did not say enough, he enclosed with the letter a draft of "Don Manuel the Lazy," dated July 1909 (and thus prior to their first meeting) wherein a heroine bears her first name: "Lilita Bengi ('I love you,' excised), you will be my wife and companion. When you die, I shall have the river Thames diverted to bury your coffin."

For there is only one thing that can counterbalance those enormous fortunes that bequeath everything to you right away: It is not talent, meticulous and slow, but, rather, genius that possesses the gift of endowing immortality. Lilita was smitten with literature as much as writers were taken with her. She preceded Giraudoux to the homes of the Du Bos at Passy, of Mr. and Mrs. Boylesve, and of Madame de Régnier (who took the pseudonym of Gérard d'Houville). Soon she would wreak havoc in the newly-formed circle of the *Nouvelle Revue française*; Léon-Paul Fargue was crazy about her.[62]

Jean lent his books to Lilita, and gave direction to her curiosity, but outside of their common friendships—Jean-Louis Vaudoyer and Martial Piéchaud among others—he did not parade any of his personal friends except for Marguerite Audoux, the little dressmaker, and Charles-Louis Philippe, who was a minor civil servant in Paris. However, he forwarded to her the sketches of his *Indifférents*, as they appeared in the journal of Gaston Gallimard and elsewhere: "Jacques the Egotist," "Don Manuel the Lazy," and "the Feeble Bernard." But he had to explain to her that he was neither indifferent, nor egotistical, nor lazy, nor feeble. For genius to be worth its weight in gold, it must include the countersignature of passion.

During the year 1912, in which the letters multiplied—occasionally three express letters on the same day—and became more tender, happier, and wittier, the love that had seemed to be mutual turned to despair for Jean, and Paul Morand told me that he had seen him in tears because of her. Maybe Lilita did not understand who he was?

Indeed, who was Jean Giraudoux? Was he the perfect lover, as perfect as Simon in the novel that he was beginning to write during this period? At that time, his heroine was christened Laura, O Petrarch! But his friend Morand recalls that Giraudoux had remained involved with an actress from the Comédie française, Wanda de Boncza, and that he occasionally had lunch with a little girl friend whom he called "Devastating Cricket," "whose ideas about history amused him":

> "Kings do not marry shepherdesses any more," she sighed.
> "You are forgetting about Louis XIV and his Maintenon," Jean riposted.
> "He married her because she had lots of money," Devastating Cricket declared confidently.[63]

And from *Simon the Pathetic:* "Everything augured well for me to marry the perfect woman very shortly. No one stopped to think I might be supporting an actress, or that a working-class girl I had deserted would kill me."[64]

Still, according to Paul Morand, Jean Giraudoux "at that time abandoned his pince-nez for a monocle, and his crew cut in favor of a part, became friends with the smart young set of the period, principally Charles de Polignac and Gilbert de Voisins, and added an element of dandyism to his characters and his stories."[65]

Was he dreaming like Suzanne—the creature of his dreams who for a while gave up the idea of ever being "anything but a lady of leisure and a multi-millionaire"? No doubt his views were divided between an assessment of the human condition (which is that of a pauper, "poor as everyone is poor, except for the wealthy")[66] and a kind of literary absolutism, close to that of fairy tales: "I pick out in my mind's eye, among the girls that I know, the most wealthy and the most beautiful, and, after having sketched her portrait, I pretend to refuse her hand."[67]

Did he give her an ultimatum, as Simon would?[68] Perhaps she told him that she was reluctant to make a love match? "I believed so sincerely that the word 'marriage,' in its simple form, is beautiful, and that the phrase 'marriage for love' is distressing."[69]

Toward the end of 1912, Jean Giraudoux could only admit his failure with respect to Lilita: "You are so much like everything that I love, everything that I revere, everything that I wish

I could have deserved" (letter of 27 December 1912). He would continue to write to her, see her, and tell her that he loved her, and that he missed her. Thereafter, she was no more than his "soul sister."

One would like to believe what he wrote to her at the happiest time of their relationship: "Had you been poor, you would still have been the way you are. Were I rich, I would still be the way I am."[70]

One week after having been shown the door by Lilita, Jean Giraudoux met the woman who was to become his wife, and, six months later, was speaking to her of marriage as something that had been decided on. Suzanne Boland was no multi-millionaire; she belonged to a good middle-class family. She had a taste for beauty and beautiful objects. Her sister was a painter, and they met in the home of the painter Baragnon. But she had little interest in literature. For him, it was a return to earth, at a time when *Simon the Pathetic* was making "giant leaps forward": "I have christened my heroine: instead of Laura, I shall call her Anne. I have made her a little less perfect. I like her more." And again: "I am breaking in a new pen-nib for you, dear Suzanne, and there is nothing more in my pen from the literature of *Simon*, whom I shall leave today to struggle between love and silence."[71]

Simon was destined for a variety of changes: it was beginning to appear in serial form when the war broke out; Giraudoux would rewrite it in 1917, publish it in 1918, then rework it twice, in 1923 and 1926. The original Anne, the heroine, would be divided among three characters in the proofs of 1918, and put back together in 1923.[72] Did it even matter that they were called Anne, Helen, and Gabrielle, since Simon spared them all "the vile task of knowing themselves"? Unpredictable like him, free of responsibilities, having their automobile and their chauffeur, their chaperone and their comforts, they are completely absorbed in their lessons of love in a park in the Ile-de-France, in a district of Paris. Their teacher is a penniless youngster, an idealistic adolescent, grown up to be this all-too-perfect young man, who, thanks to her (or to *them*), is about to experience a great but unhappy love. Or maybe not: for one who likes the pathetic, there is no such thing as an unhappy love.

Actually, the pathetic, in Simon's case, is not to be confused, as in any type of sentimental love, with the story of an unhappy love; it is first of all in the vibration engendered by a kind of writing that is totally metaphorical. The landscape, the hour, and the seasons are projected onto hearts, made suddenly somber or bright. Through the interplay of personification, apostrophe, and hyperbole, and also of ellipsis and understatement, the world echoes the characters' emotions, joyfully, mockingly, or desperately. Happiness as well as breakups are not the result of the compatibility or incompatibility of personalities, for the characters do not have personalities: there is nothing more unstable, agile, and fragile than these seekers after the absolute.

At the pinnacle of happiness, one word is enough to cast them into the abyss, the slightest "transitory and unexplainable occurrence." So at the precise moment when Anne was surrendering to tenderness, committing herself to unite with Simon as a couple until their old age, and proposing that they have "a composite name, Sianne, or Annemon for their shared telegrams," he suddenly had the feeling that she "was striving to weave false bonds" around them. Through this absurd interstice, misunderstanding insinuates itself, takes hold, and puts an end to a year that had been "exciting and uncertain."[73]

The relationship with Suzanne, his legal spouse and the mother of his only child, a son, was no easier. To see Suzanne again, says Michel Albeaux-Fernet, who was their physician and friend beginning in 1934, I have only to look at the lithograph of Daragnès that serves as frontispiece to *Anne at the Home of Simon*: there she is, this tall, brown-haired woman, with those wild eyes crying for help. She was married to a military officer. Their affair was soon discovered by the husband, who challenged his rival to a duel. Jean Giraudoux chose for his witnesses Philippe Berthelot and Paul Morand—two excellent diplomats: the duel did not take place. But the divorce came about only at the end of painful court hearings, which were prolonged due to the war and were not resolved until 20 May 1920. And as Jean was then in mourning for his father, who died on 20 February, their marriage ceremony was not performed until 5 February 1921. Moreover, Suzanne had two children, Christian and Arlette, from her first marriage, and father and mother contested the custody of the children until the divorce settlement. At one point during the war, Suzanne was hiding in a hotel so that her son would not be taken from her as her daughter had been. She was calling on Jean for assistance; Jean was either conferring with legal experts, or threatening to resort to fisticuffs. Beginning in this period, Suzanne and Jean were by turns unstable, absent, and distant, between long stretches of blissful and shared happiness. As I say "stretches," I think of beaches and of Suzanne on her Pacific island. *Suzanne and the Pacific* would appear in print in 1921, a marvelous wedding gift. In truth, the heroine of this anti-Robinson story really did not owe anything but her first name to Suzanne Boland-Giraudoux, if one is to believe Giraudoux himself. Fate had decreed that when he was a student in the middle of the province of the Beauce, he would have

> the idea of placing a young girl naked on an island. . . . Luckily, fate does a good job . . . except when it makes mistakes. . . . Wearing that uniform in which the war disguised us, so that fate could no longer distinguish us individually, there came a day when I found myself isolated in the Dardanelles, not on an island, but on a peninsula, and I was able to escape from fate. Not a single woman was there. For three months, the two hundred thousand men who were living in this little district did not see a single one, except for those who went off swimming in the night, and reached the transport ship *Annam*, anchored one nautical mile away, where there was a laundress. Her porthole was identified, and we could see her ironing.
>
> The weather was beautiful. Having returned to land, we would cut down olive trees to reinforce our trenches. . . . The ocean was of the most antique marble, veined in places with violet or green. . . . The buglers were studying the art of bugle-playing around the tomb of Achilles. . . . Each of us was caressed with a ray of sunlight that had the exact magnitude of the one that had caressed Helen. We felt the mildest of temperatures and the most heavenly of climates. It seemed as though we were applying the rouge and face powder that Helen had used. Why, suddenly, did the idea I had had in the Beauce come back to me, increased a hundred, a million times over, since instead of a single woman on an island, I saw all women in the same way, all of them, even though I had a pretty good idea of the exact census![74]

Thus, the war changed his image of woman, and women in general. They emerged from their crystal cages; they took the place of men in the fields and in the factories during the war; and they showed an unsuspected solidity. Speaking for Giraudoux, Zelten would explain it to one of them as follows: "I am no longer afraid of women! . . . My fear was due to the fact that I used to think women were rare, fragile, and perishable. War has taught me that it is in the body of a man, infinitely more vulnerable than yours, that God has lodged these magnets which attract the life-destroying lead, iron, and steel. You and all your adolescent girl friends that I used to be so afraid of touching, and then of feeling, and then of strangling, not one of you is missing in action. I shall certainly die before you; that relieves me of all my scruples."[75] And so, during the war, as a sergeant on leave and as an injured second lieutenant recovering from his two wounds, he flitted about among the nurses, those society ladies who had signed up with the Red Cross (such as Lilita, and such as the famous Misia)—without, for all that, neglecting the girls of the Cordeliers, even cutting short by a Sunday afternoon the leave that he obtained to meet Suzanne.

When he was on assignment in Portugal (September through November 1916) or in the United States (April through August 1917), he asked Paul Morand to look after the woman he already considered to be his wife: "Be very kind to her. Only be sure to avoid bringing her into contact with people who are amusing, but cynical and déclassé. She is such a neophyte! . . ."[76] However, he himself had introduced Lilita to Suzanne; and all of a sudden he discovered that Lilita perhaps preferred women to men. Hence his terror and a warning addressed to Suzanne, who had just had lunch with her:

> I am happy that she is now so kind and such a good friend, but I implore you not to flirt. Above all, don't kiss her. I have for her—and by the way, you have helped to bring this out—such a physical repulsion that the idea of your touching her upsets me. Be a good girl, chaste and innocent. I would also hate to relinquish the great friendship that I have for L. (Lilita).[77]

However, the evening when Suzanne brought Jean-Pierre Giraudoux into the world, Jean, after having sent an express letter to the clinic, had dinner with Lilita, for which Suzanne never forgave him.[78] In the end, once Lilita had married Adal Henraux, the director of national museums, the two couples maintained ties of friendship, and on his farflung missions, Jean Giraudoux did not forget to send postcards to Mr. and Mrs. Henraux.[79]

Worn out by war and the long, final illness of his father, suffering from a persistent enteritis, Jean Giraudoux, weakened and nervous, sought and found a new stability in marriage. At the time that he was moving up the ladder of the diplomatic service,[80] and his books on the war, *Campaigns and Intervals* (1917), *Amica America* (1918), *Adorable Clio* (1920), along with

Simon the Pathetic (1918) and *Elpenor* (1919), were beginning to bring him notoriety, his private life was taking shape, with a wife and a son, in a spacious old apartment near Saint-Germain-des-Prés, 8, rue du Pré-aux-Clercs.

This was the great period of his novels, begun in happiness and brought to a happy ending. *Siegfried and the Limousin* (1922) benefitted from a special advertising campaign, spiced with a mild odor of scandal due to the awarding of the Balzac Prize. Because of his dual position as novelist and diplomat, Giraudoux was the target of criticism in the campaign of Henri Béraud in 1923.[81] *Juliette in the Land of Men* (1924) kept Giraudoux, in the eyes of his readers, particularly his female readers, in the vanguard of what one critic called "literary modernism."[82]

Complete success implied happiness in marriage. However, whether his fault or hers, this period did not last long. He would have liked a quiet life, a home in which to receive his friends. But for Suzanne, the furniture was never in the right place; she wore herself out with futile rearrangements, after which his friends were entertained in a restaurant, or else she was off taking a cure. Jean was away more and more, but we also have a note—perhaps very belated—revealing the grievances Jean held against Suzanne: "I stopped by the apartment. You weren't there. I would be there more often if you were not away so much."[83]

"There once was a poor serpent who held on to all his old layers of skin. It was a man."[84] Would it be wise to try to find out how many times Jean Giraudoux shed another skin, and for which mistresses? At least twice, he would rediscover the feeling of *Simon the Pathetic*. On at least one occasion, the Lilita story would be renewed, *mutatis mutandis*.

It was in 1925, the year of the Exhibition of Decorative Arts. Women who looked like boys, with short dresses and hair, were dancing the Charleston in the smokers of the transatlantic liners. He was forty-two, and she was only sixteen as of the twelfth of March. She was dressed in astrakhan furs in order to make herself look older. She came from a wealthy neighborhood where she lived with her nanny and her chauffeur. And she had traveled an even more impressive distance. Her name was Anita de Madero, the illegitimate but recognized and beloved daughter of a father who called her "Puma" because she was so much like a little wild cat. This father belonged to the oldest aristocratic class, and one of the wealthiest and most powerful families in Argentina. As in the case of Lilita, Spanish pride and

the exoticism of the New World, along with the luxury of enormous wealth, were combined with a passion for literature.
Though raised in the convent of the Assumption, she had read
Simon the Pathetic, and, like many readers of Giraudoux, she
had wanted to meet the man behind the book. She had written
him, and he had set not only a time and place for their ren-
dezvous—in the gardens of the Trocadéro—but the way to
behave: to pretend that each was ignorant of the other's identity. . . . He was having her play out Stephy's scene on a bench
in Central Park:

> Ah! Why was it true that one day, coming straight at you from
> a narrow alleyway, appeared the one you were fated to meet! . . .
> Her blood was churning, her ears were tingling, and the noise of
> the city was taking on a special rhythm; for the first time, on this
> disc of earth that had until then been turning aimlessly, a needle
> had been set down and great bursts of sound were emanating, like
> the opening bars of a symphony.[85]

This affair would last for eleven years. Eleven years of trysts:
once or twice a week, Jean would meet Anita in the "love nest"
that she had set up for them. At most there were four or five
outings to Bourges, Arras, Amiens, and Angoulême. Even the
director Louis Jouvet did not know the identity of this beautiful
foreigner sitting by herself at a performance of *Tiger at the
Gates* in a Nina Ricci gown, a black sheath dress with two
enormous flounces—one red and the other green—and jewels
to match.

This secret life would show up in numerous places in his
works of so-called fiction, which it nourished with borrowed
memories, with whole chapters from life, and with episodes
that had been rehearsed, beginning with *Eglantine* (1927), a
novel about a young woman courted by two middle-aged men,
through *Song of Songs* (1938), which recounts the breakup between a successful entrepreneur and his young mistress, and
especially in *Combat with the Angel* (1934), in which the heroine
Maléna was modeled on Anita, along with her governess, the
governess's husband, the governess's daughter, and the beloved
Strip the Willow, who won the Jockey Prize at Chantilly—
Maléna who likewise hails from South America, land of happiness.[86]

Happiness came to an end in a twofold drama: Suzanne
learned of this affair and sank into a crisis of morbid jealousy

from which she never entirely recovered; even *Ondine* failed to move her. Had she noticed that in the final act, Hans, "stupid like a man," understood too late that he had forsaken love itself in forsaking Ondine, and how Ondine made excuses for him to the powerful Ondine King? ". . . Don't judge human feelings by our Ondine standards. Often those men who deceive their wives are the ones who are most faithful. Many deceive those whom they love so as not to be proud, to abdicate, and to feel insignificant near those who mean everything to them."[87] Didn't Suzanne understand the lesson? Did she refuse to forgive him? Being too meek and too mild, did Jean let an intolerable spouse poison his life? Or did he, through his infidelities, push an anxious wife to the brink of madness? Did he lack the courage to get a divorce, as he should have, according to their son? Was he satisfied with keeping up appearances—however badly— for his mother, his colleagues, his readers? Was he held back by religious scruples, concern for his son, or what was left of a former passion? "There will be, for all eternity, a couple named Clytemnestra and Aegisthus."[88]

There was another, more quiet drama: in February 1936, Anita returned to Argentina where she married an ambassador much like her father—an ambassador who was none other than her cousin and guardian, hardly younger than Giraudoux, just as she had promised to do several years earlier.

> No more than the Pharoah's sister, in Egypt, would have dreamed of marrying anyone other than her brother . . . would Maléna have objected to this marriage with an elderly cousin, who could prevent her turquoise mines from being diverted to the jewelry stores of New York, and who could combine them with wheat production at home.[89]

At the height of his glory, still youthful and athletic looking, and more elegant than ever, Jean Giraudoux could have rivaled his friend Morand, whom Suzanne accused with justification of wanting to "destroy their household."[90] The fact that Poupette, the younger sister of Simone de Beauvoir, had once been his mistress (which might explain Sartre's acrimony) did not prove a great deal.[91] Giraudoux was not a man of casual affairs, especially if he is to be judged by the last love of his last years.

In the spring of 1939, a young female journalist came to interview him about *Ondine*, which promised to be the greatest success of the Jouvet-Giraudoux team.[92] They saw one another again, and soon the fates of Isabelle and Jean, Jean and Isabelle (for that was the first name of the young female journalist) would be intertwined, starting, very precisely on 4 September 1939, the exact moment when the war gave an ironic significance to the new duties of Jean as Commissioner General of Information for wartime France. But at the same time that he was beginning this new romance, he was writing to "Puma" that he had agreed to speak on the radio so that she could hear him from Buenos Aires on her marvelous radio: for her guardian and husband, being an ambassador, had linked up his "wireless" (as they then called it) to the giant antenna of the Minister of Foreign Affairs, by means of two hundred meters of wire running through the embassy district. It was quite a strange time, when the Commissioner General of Information was absent from his three offices on more than one occasion: to know where he was, one would no doubt have had to question Isabelle. . . . But let us instead listen to Jean-Pierre Giraudoux:

I guessed that in the small Restaurant de la Fontaine-de-Mars, the young blond woman who was persistently staring at us was not attracted by our charms, but was curious to observe the son of her lover. A bit later, I was to have a conversation with my father on this subject. That would be the only time he would mention one of his mistresses in my presence. He promised me that he would not marry her.

Deciding that I was one of the principal causes of her arguments with my father, my mother, who was taking more initiative on my behalf, supported me in my wish to move to an apartment which would keep me at a distance. I very easily found one which I fell in love with. I had scarcely moved in when my father announced to me: "Now that you have moved out, I no longer have any reason to remain at the Quai d'Orsay." A week later, he moved into a hotel without severing ties with my mother, whose grief affected me very much and to whom I became closer. It was in a hotel that this homebody would spend his final years. . . .

My final memories of my father . . . 8 June 1940, I had lunch with him and my mother at Antonin Trémine's, at the corner of the rue Saint-Guillaume and the Boulevard Saint-Germain. That afternoon, my parents took me to Dijon where I had finally been called up. . . . That same evening, I was introduced to the colonel by my father. "Why did you shake hands with the colonel," he reproached me. "A soldier does not shake hands with his superiors." "But, Father, he extended his to me!"[93]

Father and son were not destined to meet again. Husband

and wife would continue to do so for a while, but not for very long. Following the defeat of France, Jean-Pierre deserted, and Suzanne and Jean, brought together by uncertainty, followed him to Portugal. By then, Jean-Pierre was in London, and they returned to France: "In this closed country of France in which we have hardly more than the passing of the seasons to provide us with news of our sons and of our absent gods. . . ." That was the first sentence of *Without Powers*.

From that time on, he would spend more time living in Vichy, about three kilometers from his mother, than in Paris, where, moreover, he would stay at a hotel rather than in his apartment. At long intervals, the couple would come together for an occasional dinner in an attempt to keep up appearances in the eyes of the world. But Jean would leave with the last of the invited guests.

As for Isabelle, she was free with a bizarre kind of freedom: her husband was a prisoner of war, and she lived in the region of Lyon, on the other side of the occupied zone. Jean and Isabelle kept in touch through interzone postcards, mailed without envelopes. He signed with female first names, hiding his identity under the names of Jeanne Morel or Madame Colombe: "Returned to the hotel and am now writing you before even changing my dress." He tried to convince her that she was his muse, that she was "the true Isabelle," and he dedicated to her a draft of *The Apollo of Marsac*: "To you who have taught me that I am handsome."[94]

To "the true Isabelle," he would never promise marriage, "that is to say, the least expression of love."[95] Didn't the other Isabelle, the one in *Intermezzo*, say to her fiancé:

> Take me in your arms, Roland. But if your only purpose is to take me away from everything that is calling out to me, to make me refuse all those other invitations beyond this world, to recast the two of us into what all other couples are, our faces for mirrors, only our two backs turned to the rest of the universe, that poor human blockade. . . .[96]

Isabelle was very devout, and Jean used Notre-Dame des Victoires as an intercessor. He called her by every name to bring her closer—this woman who was young enough to be his daughter: "To my sister Isabelle, to my daughter Isabelle, to Isabelle." They met in Vienna, mostly in Lyon, occasionally in Barbotan—

brief encounters for trysts, sometimes happily despite the circumstances.

Sodom and Gomorrah was evoking the end of the world as the bombings, which were becoming more and more frequent, were concomitantly presenting visions of the apocalypse. But in Giraudoux's play, the end of the world has been caused by the end of the human couple, the total lack of understanding between the sexes. Man and woman each possess their own language and their own truth. An infinite despair prolongs this interminable domestic conflict raised to the level of biblical tragedy. At a dress rehearsal, a very young actor, Gérard Philipe, made his début in the role of the Angel: "But Lia, please try to understand. There has never been a creature. There has never been anything but the couple."[97] Those in the auditorium were stunned. Close friends noticed one evening that Suzanne was in the audience. Had it been written for her, this oratorio of dissension, this tribute transcending all breakups, all infidelities, and all lacerations? Isabelle suddenly came to the conclusion that the play was dedicated to the spouse, and that she herself had only been the mistress of a worn-out man, not the muse of the writer of genius. She broke it off. Jean protested: "Let imbeciles see in the song of the couple the song of marriage; that's their privilege. But that what has been written in a legend should be turned against itself—that gives me infinite pain—on top of all my other pain. . . . Thank you, Angel." In vain. "Why you have destroyed everything with a single gesture, I still cannot fathom." Isabelle did not answer. Three months later, he was dead.*

Through an error that is common for the literary historian, this last play to be presented while he was still alive has been often considered as a last testament. French audiences still did not know *The Apollo of Bellac*, which Jouvet had opened in Rio de Janeiro in 1942,[98] and even less, *The Madwoman of Chaillot* and its invitation to love: "Kiss him, Irma. If two human beings who love each other let a single minute come between them, it turns into months, years, and centuries."[99] Still less, *For Lucrece*, the glorification of a heroine exemplifying the qualities Giraudoux admired—youth, beauty, and purity—and which

---

*Translator's Note: These excerpts from Giraudoux's letter to Isabelle have been cited by Laurent Le Sage and Lucie Heymann in *Les Cahiers*, no. 8 (1979), p. 55.

would not be staged (by Jean-Louis Barrault and Madeleine Renaud) until 1953.

As for the numerous texts in which woman took her place alongside man, as a friend and an equal, they had no doubt been forgotten. Refer first to the little booklet on *Sports*:

> Sports are synonymous with chastity.
> Athletic women consider men to be their friends.
> They exclude flirtation and artifice when they are with them.
> They consider love to be friendship.
> They give themselves in friendship to him, to them.[100]

Next, and most prominently, a series of lectures delivered in 1934–35 at the University of Annals, which would not be collected for publication by his heirs until 1951, under the title *The Frenchwoman and France*. The original titles were: "Woman in 1934," "Women Take Over," and "Woman Face to Face With the Universe." In addition to these was a lecture delivered when Giraudoux was Commissioner General of Information: "Regarding Saint Catherine" (24 November 1939).

Beginning in 1934, Giraudoux, acknowledging the failure of the French people, called for women to take over from men, and spoke unequivocally in favor of the equality of men and women, especially in the labor market; he called for women's right to vote and, more generally, he advocated "brightening, adding dignity to, and improving the status of women in the world." Already, through the character of Geneviève Prat, a sculptress, in *Siegfried and the Limousin*, or that of Isabelle, the little schoolteacher who stood up to the Inspector in *Intermezzo*, he recognized that women have "an unbiased understanding of the world, and no notion of the impossible."[101] In *Tiger at the Gates*, the group of women is Hector's strongest support in his struggle against the stupidity of men. Electra is a new Louise Michel, another Pasionaria, while Clytemnestra is perhaps the first militant for women's liberation.

At around the same time, Giraudoux was paying respect to the new audience of women spectators and also to the women readers for whom he had always been writing.[102] He invited them to come and see him just as Juliette had done, since it was in her honor that he had broken through the paper hoop of his fiction and declared himself in his "Prayer on the Eiffel Tower." He told them about their magical power over men and

over the world. He spoke to them about themselves in a way
that was both intimate and restrained, with a veiled eroticism.
He revealed to them that "each one carries in her heart something which makes us desire them all."[103] He invited them to
love him and to love.

But he also told them that "the worst misunderstanding is
to love";[104] that only a huge stretch of the imagination could
lead one to believe "that it was the god of beauty himself who
visited you this morning,"[105] and that love is more upsetting
than any dream of love: "For if Stephy was determined to reckon
on that man's absence for the rest of her life, she had never
as yet imagined that he might be present. . . ."[106] He told them
that love is carnage: "One should make love only on a ship,
or a raft; you let go of it, afterwards, then the rest of the world
is unharmed. . . ."[107] He was finding out for himself at the same
time that he was informing them about the price of love: "it's
always costly."[108] He also told them, in the words of Ondine:
"The more one suffers, the happier one is. I am happy. I am
the happiest one alive." Along with the words of wisdom: "A
bit too much. If one begins to love like that in this life, well,
that doesn't make things easier. . . ."[109]

He suggested as well that between a man and a woman some
less passionate ties be established, ones that are more natural,
and more purely carnal. He imagined, for fun, enchanted islands
where women gave themselves without either jealousy or puri-
tanism.[110] He told them what Holofernes had told Judith:

> Think how sweet your day would be, free of fears and of prayers.
> Think of your morning breakfast served without the threat of hell,
> and of five-o'clock tea without mortal sin, with a beautiful piece
> of lemon and innocent, shiny sugar tongs. Think of the young men
> and young women easily embracing each other between cool sheets,
> and tossing pillows at each other's head, with pink heels kicking,
> without angels or demons spying on them. . . ![111]

Helen, the first star of humanity—and "humanity owes as much
to its stars as it does to its martyrs"—offers an example of this
physical purity:

> "You do not love Paris, Helen. You love men!"
> "I don't deny it. It's enjoyable to rub them against you like big
> bars of soap. You feel completely purified by them. . . ."[112]

To those, and to her (Andromache), who pretend that this

pure pleasure of lovemaking is not love at all, Helen might answer:

> You are hard to please. . . . I don't think my kind of love is all that bad. I like it. Obviously, it does not affect my liver or my spleen when Paris leaves me to go bowling or to fish for eel. But I am ruled by him, and magnetized by him. Magnetization is as much love as is promiscuity. It is a passion much older and much more productive than the one that is expressed by eyes that are red from crying, or which shows itself by physical contact. I am just as comfortable in this kind of love as a star in its constellation. I gravitate to it; I sparkle within it; that's my way of breathing and of embracing. One may easily foresee the sons that this kind of love could produce: big, bright beings, very distinct with ringed fingers and short noses. What will happen to my love if I inject into it jealousy, tenderness, and anxiety! The world is already so nervous: just see for yourself![113]

Helen found in Paris the partner that suited her, one who loved distant women (but from up close) and who would willingly exchange them: "Love includes some truly exhilarating moments; those are the breakups"; and who, in a gently amoral way, makes fun of romantic and Lamartinian love: "Only one being is absent and everything is repopulated. . . . All women are created anew for you; all belong to you, and what's more, in freedom, dignity, and a quiet conscience. . . ."[114]*

Judith without Jehovah, Don Juan without the Commandant, women without symbols, men without a past, love without imagination? Giraudoux sought in vain to discover a new art of loving which would avoid both crystallization and idealization, the romantic and the tragic. He came up only with characters of comedy: Agatha, Dalila. In his final works, *Ondine, Sodom and Gomorrah, The Madwoman of Chaillot,* and *For Lucrece,* he returned to the early myth of androgyny, of absolute union, of the fusion between two beings as the sole ideal of love and, failing that, to a permanent physical embrace between man and woman, since "in love only presence counts."[115] What was no more than a mania in the case of sweet Lotte, "to be attached, not only through a lively feeling, nor through a lively appetite, but by a real attachment, a belt or chain, to the one she loved,"[116] becomes Ondine's ideal[117] and the "strips of flesh" reappear

---

*Translator's Note: The specific reference here is to Lamartine's poem "L'isolement": "Un seul être vous manque, et tout est dépeuplé!"

in *Sodom and Gomorrah*[118] as if to affirm that there is no other love, and that only a woman knows how to love:

> *The Angel.* God did not create man and woman one after the other, nor one from the other. He created two twin bodies joined by strips of flesh that he subsequently cut through, in a confident mood, the day he created affection. . . .
>
> *Lia.* Then, make the strips of flesh over again. So that Jean and I could open up in the morning, and close together in the evening, like a book.

6

THE PRESENCE OF ONE NOW ABSENT

I am recalling one who is absent, who, even when he was living, was absent. The first scene is set in Saint-Amand-Montrond, around 1892, a little earlier or a little later. Jean was either eight or eleven years old. He was vacationing at the home of his maternal aunt, in this mecca of culture (compared to the modest village of Pellevoisin where his parents kept their older son under their watchful eye). In Saint-Amand-Montrond, he discovered, at the home of an elderly professor, the art of drawing, and, at the home of neighbors, the toys of rich children as well as that rare and expensive commodity, books. He also discovered the art of theater, as would be related by his cousin Renée Lacoste, two or three years his elder:

> When there were visiting theatrical companies, concerts, or shows by local amateurs, we would take our cousin along with us. He adored them and as soon as we returned home, before we had finished lighting the oil lamps or candles and preparing refreshments, Jean had already disappeared. We would find him under the kitchen table, devouring a book despite the poor lighting. He did not waste a minute.[1]

Thirty years later, during the years 1924–26, Jean Giraudoux was the head of the press bureau of the Ministry of Foreign Affairs. He had two daily meetings—at noon and at seven o'clock—with the French and foreign press. But the ministers would neglect to brief him, and so he would have to give the journalists something to chew on, based upon rumors and an occasional dispatch from the agency. But on this particular day, he had not been seen all morning, and at noon, his deputy Pierre Bressy was obliged to cope with the journalists in his

stead. The day wore on without his making an appearance.
Already that morning there had been several phone calls for
him, in particular, from the minister's chambers. He was supposed to phone back. Another call came, and Pierre Bressy asked
the callers to wait while he phoned on another line: "Is Mr.
Giraudoux in your office?" "Is Mr. Giraudoux at home?" "Is
Jean at your house?" The situation seemed hopeless, and Bressy
was getting tangled up in the wires of his two telephones when
he caught sight of his department head grinning at him through
the half-open door: "I see you are working beyond the call of
duty!"[2] It would be a mistake to conclude from this incident
that he was a bad official. Both in the service des oeuvres and
in the press bureau, he made his mark.* His career was brilliant
and his advancement extremely rapid, despite the distrust that
Raymond Poincaré and, later, Alexis Léger (alias Saint-John
Perse) had of him. Undeniably, he knew how to keep a sense
of proportion vis-à-vis administrative routine.

Fifteen years later, Jean Giraudoux was at the pinnacle of
his success. His latest play, Ondine, had been better attended
even than Maurice Chevalier.[3] In the windows of all the bookstores, there was a new novel, Choice of the Elect, and a political
essay, Full Powers. At this juncture, the newspapers announced
his appointment as Commissioner General of Information. Alas!
There could be no doubt about it; he would be expected to
be in charge of France's wartime propaganda, for a war that
was almost certainly inevitable. One more time, he would be
called on to inform without being informed, to justify a political
policy, and to explain a strategy, without taking part either
in the Council of Ministers or in the Council of War. The journalists believed him to be responsible for the censorship, which
in fact was outside his control. It was an impossible situation.
His offices were set up in a wing of the Continental Hotel,
part of which had been requisitioned. Pursued by interviewers
and petitioners, he would escape by means of the hotel stairway;
he also maintained an office at the Quai d'Orsay, and he had
a third in the Prime Minister's chambers. There would be a

---

*Translator's Note: The service des oeuvres has no equivalent in American
government and bureaucracy. This rubric of French "works" included hospitals, public schools and universities at home, and a variety of service institu-
tions abroad. The most important branch of the service des oeuvres was the
department of education, particularly French schools abroad, which was Giraudoux's chief responsibility prior to directing the total network of the service
des oeuvres.

phone call. It might be from the President of the Republic or from his wife Suzanne. He was not to be found in any of his three offices.

On the art of disappearing and its mastery as perfected by Jean Giraudoux, one of his colleagues of the period, André Beucler, has related numerous anecdotes. A scholarly, even pedantic woman who was trying to monopolize his attention told him: "You are perhaps a bit too Eutychian." His response was: "Oh! Not at all. I am evasion incarnate, and I can prove it to you on the spot." And he did.

At the entrance to a restaurant, a bore accosted him: "You once wrote, my dear sir. . . ." Giraudoux responded absently while heading to the table where Beucler was waiting for him.

> "I see that someone is waiting for you, Mr. Minister, and I apologize for bothering you, but I would like to ask you one last question, the classic and perfidious question . . ."
> "What time do you have dinner?"
> "No," replied the stranger, blushing. "Rather: Why do you write?"
> "To escape," said Giraudoux with emphasis.
> "To escape," repeated the stranger pensively. "To escape from whom?"
> "To escape, to escape . . . just as I am doing right now."[4]

Who can boast of having been in his confidence? He deployed, recalls André Beucler, "an ingenious and obstinate Machiavellianism in being the one who asks the questions, never the one who answers them." And Denise Tual similarly observes: "At around eleven o'clock, having finished part of his work, he would venture out into Paris on one of his mysterious walks that he kept secret. . . . We never knew where he went."

Some of his absences have the appearance of a desertion. In view of the fact that, beginning in 1922, he had called for Franco-German reconciliation while at the same time pointing out how virulent the militaristic spirit still was beyond the Rhine, and how dangerous the desire for revenge,[5] why, in the thirties, was he silent, and why did he not belong to the Committee of Antifascist Intellectuals? In December 1935, after the preview performance of *Tiger at the Gates*, *L'Humanité* answered in his stead: "If, to the disappointment of certain individuals, Jean Giraudoux has refrained from joining the demonstrations which have been taking place for or against peace or culture, it is perhaps because the writer was waiting to take a stand in his own fashion."[6]

In London, in the quarters of General de Gaulle, in July 1940, when a telegram arrived from Lisbon signed Giraudoux, they expected the author of *Adorable Clio*. But it was his son who arrived, who having found himself so destitute that, given the price per word for international telegrams, he had been unable to pay for a first name. As the weeks, months, and years passed, the son's invitations to his father to join him were in vain. But after the opening of *Sodom and Gomorrah* in October 1943, the strongest of the "collaborationist" Parisian newspapers, *Je suis partout*, made note of the presence of "all those gentlemen of the de Gaulle literary coterie, who had apparently made a special trip back from London."[7]

Giraudoux himself was aware of his absences. Sometimes he was like the one baptised by Stephy as the Shadow: "He was a shadow because he was covered with a coating and a kind of absence which nothing could grab onto."[8] And after the defeat of 1940, when in less than twelve months he was obliged to go from the pinnacle of his glory to the nadir of humiliation, "from the furthest reaches of hope to the furthest reaches of defeat," he absented himself spiritually: "It was as if my shadow had taken over for me." His *double* had driven his car through the fleeing masses; his double experienced defeat and its corollaries; and his double was there when "the National Assembly called for its own defeat." He witnessed the collapse of the Republic. But he himself experienced nothing, saw nothing, and knew nothing. "For myself, I know that I feel nothing, that I wish to feel nothing, and that I am preserving my strength or my weakness by I know not what means, by slow death, or by keeping it on ice."[9]

To be there *(Dasein)*, say the existential philosophers. Isn't being elsewhere just another way of being there? "Electra is never more absent than from the place where she is."[10] The Madwoman of Saint-Sulpice walks around with "a kind of guest whose name she has not even told us and who certainly exists only in her imagination." The Madwoman of Chaillot retorts: "If you can't accept that as existence. . . ."[11] Giraudoux knew and practiced absence as a way of being present elsewhere.

"The only remedy for shadow is dazzling light."[12] How clear everything would become in the light of God! Did Giraudoux believe in God? And anyway, what is the difference between believing and not believing? Between "not believing" like the

Inspector in *Intermezzo*, who challenges spirits in whom he does not believe to reveal their existence while he calls on each of them by name and denounces their individual vices,[13] and "believing" in the manner of Aegisthus:

> I believe in the gods. Or rather, I believe that I believe in the gods. But I believe in them not as great manifestations of attentiveness or supervision, but as a great absent-mindedness. Always flirting between space and time, forever locked in a struggle between gravitation and emptiness, there are great masses of indifference, that are the gods.

What better proof of their existence can they give to the Gardener in *Electra* ("All of them up there, as many as there are, and even if there is no more than one of them, and even if that one is absent") than their silence? "As for me, I've always found the silences the most convincing."[14] Fontranges had already explained to Jerome Bardini that "God's punishments are invisible. Therein lies their greatness. They affect neither our happiness nor our conscience. They are a moment of silence from God."[15]

Should one turn then to humans? "Humans, the supreme mildew of the universe," as Eglantine remarks?[16] "That supreme and mobile mildew of the earth that is humanity," as Aegisthus remarks?[17]

> Come now, you've seen them, . . . you have learned since then how they are made, right? You have seen them? You have seen those doleful flat areas at their temples, those pumice stone cheeks, worn away as if from birth they had spent their lives rubbing against other temples and other cheeks?[18]

When Sartre, both in his criticism and in his tribute, saw fit to sum up Giraudoux in the word *humanism*, he must have been blinded by his desire to paint, as has been observed, "a mirror image of Sartre himself," or, rather, to eliminate the long shadow of Giraudoux by shedding light on his other side, which does indeed exist although it is much less pronounced: a kind of resignation to humanity? In the words of Alcmena:

> Since your Jupiter, rightly or wrongly, has created death on the earth, I throw my lot in with that of my planet. I am too aware of all the fibers of my being as extensions of those of other humans, animals, even of plants, not to link my fate with theirs. . . . To become immortal, for a human being, is to betray.[19]

And the most human of all will be Ondine, daughter of the waters, who enters into humanity by love and by choice.[20] But, to tell the truth—the truth of the Inspector of *Intermezzo*, the truth of human reason, a serpent stinging its own tail, the truth of human language, that is, nonsense: "Humanity is a superhuman enterprise."[21] If there is one feeling alien to Giraudoux, it is pride in being human.

"Pride is all that remains to us from original sin," he wrote in a text entitled "Pride."[22] This fact is amusing when one considers that Paul Morand never knew a man as proud as Giraudoux.[23] One could even add: nor one as thin-skinned, when one considers how he reacted to the critiques of *Judith* (in the "Discourse on Theater") and of *Electra* (in *The Paris Impromptu*).[24] But his enormous pride, at being first, at being the glory of the Limousin, at being handsome, at being perfect, or at least not entirely imperfect, like Simon ("One single imperfection, I sensed, would have compromised everything about me. So, I tried not to have any"),[25] his "angelism," as it was called, is also a confession of indignity, a regret at being neither patient "like the trees waiting for the rain," nor peaceful like the plants, each in its own space, nor faithful to his nature like the animals.[26] He was very elegant—actually, too elegant, in the words of André Chamson, who, during the "phoney war," saw him arrive at his quarters, a commissioner general on a special assignment. But one had to realize that he had his clothes made in London for want of being the Apollo of Bellac, who can be seen only with one's eyes closed:

> My height is one and a half times the height of a human. My head is small and weighs one seventh of my body weight. The idea of the right angle came to mathematicians from my shoulders, and the idea of the bow came to Diana from my eyebrows. I am naked, and the idea of breastplates came to the goldsmiths from this nudity.[27]

Giraudoux proud? "You know very well what I mean. Pride is not vanity. It is a feeling of nausea at the thought of Creation, of disgust for our way of life, a flight from our dignities, and it is a terrible modesty." And Giraudoux was modest, almost timid to the point of blushing when he was the subject of conversation.[28] In two or three places in his work, he even implies that no one exceeds him in modesty.

"Are you proud of being a man?"

"No," said Bardini. "But neither can I imagine any other creature in whose skin I would be proud of living."[29]

He was in the same situation as Mozart on his deathbed, hiding from his wife that *Requiem* which "was threatened by everything in the human race. . . . And yet to what other race could it be entrusted?"[30] Not that the name of Mozart should impress us too much: "In point of fact, no man is a genius. . . . A humanity made up only of men of genius would simply be a humanity without imbeciles. If I were Dante and Claude Bernard, I would be almost as ashamed as I am of being Bardini."[31] So thought Juliette now and then, "with the impression that our planet is still having labor contractions, and that mankind is a kind of insect," "disgusted, as no human before her had been, with clothes, door latches, and articulate speech," Juliette "of an interstellar nature"; Juliette "the Parisian woman of the firmament."[32] And yet we see her venturing into the land of men.

For Giraudoux did not need to be committed in the way that Sartre advocated after having himself missed all the boats in history. He was already committed, ready to set sail with the men of his generation, and, as far as it was within his power, most often at the outposts and the prow. In 1905, while the French and German empires were clashing in Morocco, he was heading to Munich, hoping "to press for the restitution of Alsace."[33] In 1908, in the United States, witnessing the assiduous wooing of American universities by official representatives of German culture, he conceived the subject matter of one of his first diplomatic notes,[34] as well as the idea of propaganda for France (and in the French style) which would later become the major theme of his career in the *service des oeuvres*, in the press relations department, as General Inspector of Diplomatic Posts, and, of course, as Commissioner General of Information, but also of his lectures on the French woman (1934–35), on the French "problem" (1939), and, after his retirement, of what he had "written in darkness" under the title *Without Powers*. All of which explains why he was picked to go to Harvard in 1917—not on the same ship as Bergson, as is recounted in *Amica America*, but in his wake—when, at all costs, France needed to bring the United States into the war alongside her.[35] And he who arrogantly proclaimed, "I am a conquerer on Sundays at noon," could no doubt be accused of nationalism.[36] But

how many people are aware that, as early as 1921, he promised
Grasset a pamphlet on *French Imperialism?* National susceptibil-
ities, it is true, were cleverly spared in *Siegfried and the
Limousin* (1922). Nonetheless, this plea for a renewal of intellectual entente between France and Germany, coming from a writer
of the extreme avant-garde, but one with a foothold in French
diplomacy, was like a swallow announcing the summer; giving
heart, for instance, to a number of students from the Ecole
Normale Supérieure clustered around Robert Minder, who were
holding pacifist discussions, taking up collections for the children of unemployed Germans, and inviting to the rue d'Ulm
German writers who were forbidden to speak at the Sorbonne
because they were German, even if their names were Hofmannsthal or Heinrich Mann.[37] Written in the same spirit as *Bella*
(1926), *Siegfried* was praised as a political event, an "intellectual
Locarno," and unleashed a "*Siegfried* controversy" which dou-
bled its acclaim. René Doumic, "with a heavy heart and a profound feeling of sadness and humiliation," accused Giraudoux
of having written "a play in honor of Germany," and of having
shown and sung "on a French stage . . . the German military
uniform . . . the German national anthem!" (for this is how bad
things were). The foolishness of the old academician, but also
Giraudoux's cleverness, were such that he was defended not
only by the left-wing newspapers but even by Lucien Dubech,
the critic for *Action française,* who seemed to be trying to make
amends for having once called him the worst writer of his generation. Giraudoux profited by not having to respond to Doumic,
merely confiding to a reporter: "There are some things that you
simply can't do to someone who is your neighbor" (they both
lived on the rue du Pré-aux-Clercs).[38]

His most extreme views on nationalism remain unpublished.
In the tragedy *The Gracchi,* which he never completed, although
he reworked it several times, one of the characters said: "There
was a time when I believed in nations."[39] But what he did publish beginning in the same year (1936) shows that he essentially
stopped presenting problems in terms of foreign policy, having
become convinced that the enemy was not outside but within.
A great deal of ignorance, or of bad faith, is needed to accuse
Giraudoux, as has occasionally been done, of lacking lucidity
when, in the introduction to *Full Powers* in the spring of 1939,
he wrote that his "greatest worry was not on account of Germany
or Italy." After the *Anschluss,* Munich, and the Sudentenland,
no one doubted the threat of Hitler any longer. Did this mean

that one should "blame Germany and Italy, who are in no way responsible, for a fatal affliction that is strictly internal"?[40] Didn't the catastrophe derive from the inability of Western democracies to define a policy other than that of vacillating between Berlin and Moscow, which led to the reversal of alliances and to the slaughter? Didn't the French army in May and June of 1940, seem to have succumbed as much to an internal disintegration as to the attacks of the Blitzkrieg? The danger was from within, in the functioning of French society and in the monopolization of the machinery of the state by certain factions and certain classes. It has rarely been acknowledged how clearly Giraudoux unequivocally implicated the two hundred families in *The Gracchi*: "Two hundred families who accumulate lucrative jobs and bribes, whose understanding of business is limited to profit and routine."[41] And in *The Madwoman of Chaillot*: "No order will be respected by the members of the two hundred families! and no laws!"[42] And also in *Full Powers* where he accused the "grim" men of bribing municipal counselors, if not members of parliament and ministers as well.[43] The denunciation of the two hundred families—the principal shareholders of the French National Bank—was one of the major themes of the Popular Front. But Giraudoux was publishing his articles on domestic policy, from 1935 to 1937, in *Le Figaro*, which was militantly opposed to the Popular Front. . . . To convince the opposition, rather than preach to the converted; to transcend partisan divisions: such was his way, such was his ambition—or his illusion.

Having become, little by little, a "writer-journalist,"[44] he began by doing sports commentaries, and went from there to the concept of city planning. It was a longtime preoccupation, for one of the heroes of his second book was already contemplating the rebuilding of Paris.[45] *School for the Indifferent* appeared in 1911, when the very idea of city planning was in its infancy. He had as a friend Raoul Dautry beginning in 1918, and around 1928, Le Corbusier, who had great admiration for him and dedicated to him his *Radiant City*, still in manuscript. He had known Germany, whose architectural schools shaped the twentieth century. He had known Jean Forestier (not to be confused with Jacques Forestier, the French name of Siegfried in the stage version of the novel; Jean Forestier was the prophetic but very real name of a French landscape architect mentioned in *Siegfried and the Limousin*[46] and whom he mentions in *Full Powers* at the beginning of the chapter entitled "Modern France: Our Life"). A student of the Ecole Polytechnique, upon his graduation, Forestier wanted to join the navy, but was forced back to the land by an arcane ruling.* "He knew why he was drawn instinctively to the sea: it was because men cannot pollute it." Those were the days before oilslicks!

> This creator . . . was called on by our civil service only to be given the wholly inappropriate title of curator.** He was, when I knew him, curator of the parks of Paris. Indeed, he cared for them well. He lived in the heart of the Bois de Boulogne. . . . He did not like the country. "I am a true man of the cities," he said. "I love the open air and gardens." For that was his definition of a city.[47]

Together they founded in 1928 the "Urban League" (later the "Urban and Rural League for Environmental Planning of French Life"). Jean Forestier was president and Jean Giraudoux was vice president; one of the founding members was Raoul Dautry, and their manifesto was entitled: "In Defense of the Beauty and the Health of Paris."[48] Forestier's death interrupted the work of the League, which was revived in 1933, by an article that Giraudoux signed with his title of vice president, as he did several others that followed, in *Marianne* and then in *Le Figaro*. He put his finger on the "abscesses" of Paris, problems of his time, but ones which were not resolved until after the war, if then: the transfer of the Halles and of the wine market, the restoration of historical sites, the protection of green spaces, relieving congestion around the gates of Paris. He deplored the seizure of the fortification zone by "private enterprise," "the accumulation of garbage dumps and housing developments in the forests and parks of the suburbs." He cited as examples of good planning the garden cities of Suresnes, the city hall of Puteaux, and Villeurbanne, where, in a new quarter, the socialist town council had built a town hall, a community center for the workers, and a temple truly Giralducien in inspiration: a theater with an underground swimming pool. He did not cast on the authorities the entire blame for the disorder that he witnessed: Parisians must take some of the blame, he said, and

---

*Translator's Note: The arcane ruling, which derived from the seventeenth century, required a degree of muscular development that Forestier did not possess; consequently, he was rejected for service.

**Translator's Note: The French word *conservateur* has a double meaning, not only that of curator or guardian, but of *conservative*, that is, the opposite of creative.

the purpose of the urban league was to group together individual initiatives that were scattered in too many directions.

What was the doctrine that impelled Sir Giraudoux, defender of city planning? His motto included three words. First, *freedom*, but not the freedom to demolish, to disfigure, to exploit, and to speculate; these kinds of freedom are to be found everywhere, and Jean Giraudoux deplored them. Freedom, or, rather, what he terms "urban freedom" or "urban rights," he defines as follows:

> The rights which the citizen has with regard to the city. He has the right to a sound body and to a lifestyle that enables him to enjoy both work and leisure as he deserves. . . . Every citizen, regardless of the class he is from, has the right to the same health, to the same leisure activities, to the same freedom to come and go: each district ought to furnish him the same amenities and beauty as the districts which used to be called upper-class neighborhoods.[49]

Freedom, followed by *equality:*

> Let's not talk of heaven; the way to achieve that is not a matter for debate. But since each man has a claim to the Earth, and each citizen has a claim to his Country, like all other human beings and citizens, there is only one humane and national policy, which lies in the goal of making the expression of this equality easy and real for him. To every child that is born, the nation owes the same welcoming gift: that of the nation itself, in its totality, and without limitations.[50]

Giraudoux never owned property, not even his own apartment. In the conflict that is eternally latent between landlords and tenants, he had taken sides: for the house. For the land of men, rather than for men themselves. Men, after all, are only worthy of "this beautiful name of man" if they respect the other species, their planet, and, through them, the future.

Hence, the third word, at the risk of disappointing, is not fraternity. Giraudoux was not very gifted at demonstrations of emotion. Urbanity is a word which would suit him better, since it indicates a respect for distances. The third word of Giraudoux's motto is *imagination;* it is *creation;* it is *invention.* The task of conservation goes hand in hand with the task of construction. Giraudoux was, like his Holofernes, "the friend of well-tended gardens and well kept houses," and France seemed to him to be a nation that was "badly kept."[51] He dubbed himself the water diviner of the garden of Eden, which he saw as being ahead in the future. Referring to the Gardener of *Electra* and to the Gardener of *Sodom and Gomorrah*, he liked to say jokingly: "In this world where I have no garden, I have at least a gardener that follows me around."[52] A gardener that kept running through his head to the point of giving him the appearance of being absent, but who allows him to be present today, and perhaps tomorrow, if man will just stop behaving like the "jockey of the planet," whipping his mount along as if he could exchange it for another. "The chief occupation of humanity is nothing but a universal enterprise of demolition. I mean, of course, the male of the species."[53] So spoke the Madwoman of Chaillot, and through the delirium of her imagination, one can recognize the affirmation of what Giraudoux called his "mission": "the affirmation of the future, the negation of the present."[54] We have to make a decision, the Madwoman explains to her friends, which will transform the world "and turn it into a paradise."[55] As the enemy of oil prospectors and the protectress of animals, she is a spokesperson for Giraudoux the prophet of ecology and the protector of picturesque sites and historical buildings.

In the fall of 1940, Giraudoux was named Director of Historical Landmarks, a consolation prize which failed to please him, since he proceeded to assert his right to retire.[56] Nevertheless, he attempted to interest the Marshal (Pétain) in his idea of city planning, without success.[57] When the Liberation came, the government of General de Gaulle, on the other hand, included for the first time a minister of Reconstruction *and City Planning*, who was Giraudoux's friend, Raoul Dautry.

Not the least of the paradoxes is the fact that Jean Giraudoux, to begin with, had meant to devote his life, upon the advice of his family (I am not inventing this; it is a quotation) "to the Vichy-Etat Company."[58] A cousin of his mother's, Alexandre Sabourdy, whom he called uncle, was director of the plant that manufactured Vichy tablets.* During the time when the entire middle class was plagued with liver problems, Vichy was the summer meeting place *par excellence* for people of distinction, some seeking the cure, and others staying at the administrative

---

*Translator's Note: The Vichy *pastilles* are peppermint-flavored, chalky tablets primarily intended for the relief of indigestion. Vichy-Etat is the name of the firm that prepares them.

headquarters of the Company of the Vichy Springs, both groups departing with their supply of Vichy tablets. The young graduate student was introduced by his uncle Sabourdy to Gaston Calmette, the editor of *Le Figaro*, who procured for him the press card that came in so handy in Munich and at Harvard, and undoubtedly through the same connection, it fell to him to act as a guide through Munich for no less than Joseph Caillaux himself, who had once been Minister of Finance and would be reappointed the following year. Gaston Calmette may in turn have recommended Giraudoux to Maurice Bunau-Varilla, the editor of *Le Matin*.

It was indeed in Vichy, but not at all on account of the Company of the Vichy Springs, nor in the service of the French government that in 1941, Giraudoux collected his principal articles of literary criticism in a volume that was to receive the title *French Literature*, a profession of patriotism in the midst of the Occupation, but also a declaration of war on the middle class. Already in his article on the centennial of *Hernani* (1930), he had accused Romanticism of having been in league with "the selfish and moneyed classes," and in his article on Charles-Louis Philippe (1937), he denounced "monopolization of expression by a middle-class caste." In the preface to *Literature*, he explains how "the writer and the written word became the property of the ruling caste, to wit, of the middle class," and, since "the middle class does not like to pick up stones under which there are sleeping serpents," the "literary middle class" saw itself scorned by the "ruling middle class" without, however, getting a hearing from "all the lower classes" and from "all those who are workers, from the peasant to the artisan." No doubt this attack on the middle class, as well as this salute to the workers, were commonplaces of political oratory. However, the fact remains that among the articles mourning Giraudoux's death figured two long testimonials, one of which was signed Brasillach and the other Aragon. Giraudoux, throughout his life, made many friends, was envied by quite a few, but had very few enemies. To claim that he was a collaborator is even more untrue than to claim that he had joined the Resistance. It is true that beginning in September 1940, he wrote to his son: "Our mission is to resist with all our hearts since we have not been allowed to resist with all our weapons," but he was not in a position to resist in any way other than by the pen. Thus, the theory that the Germans or the militia poisoned him is quite improbable. He was carried away in three days by blood poisoning, but it was undoubtedly caused by food, which may be explained by the wretched cooking of the wretched restaurants of this wretched time.[59] Because of the circumstances, his family and the doctors bypassed the ban to inter him, which would have authorized an autopsy but would also have attracted the attention of the Gestapo, who at the time had already detained Christian Pineau, his stepson, while his own son was sailing in the free French naval forces.

His political testament was couched in the manuscript of *Without Powers*, in which he had deleted references to Marshal Pétain, and which had gradually become a dossier of France at the time of the Liberation, and also in the manuscript of *The Madwoman of Chaillot*, on which he had written (apparently, for the page has disappeared): "This play was produced by the company of Louis Jouvet at the Athénée Theatre, 17 October 1945."[60] The prophecy came within two months of being accurate: Jouvet, returning from South America after the Liberation, produced *The Madwoman of Chaillot* on 21 December 1945, a gala performance in honor of the "Members of the Resistance of 1940," attended by General de Gaulle. Another political testament was the unfinished manuscript of *The Gracchi* wherein two brothers' views of the colonial policy conducted by their native Rome are opposed:

> *Tiberius.* She owns the world. And, throughout, she disseminates justice and happiness.
> *Caius.* She massacres, she corrupts, and she pillages.[61]

The Gracchi was published for the first time in the middle of the Algerian war (1958) in *L'Express*, which underscored its contemporary relevance. In *Full Powers*, in *The Gracchi*, and in *The Madwoman of Chaillot* (and even as early as *Intermezzo*), there was a recurring dread of the regimentation of cultures throughout the planet and of individuals throughout society, a major threat to the anticonformist that Giraudoux himself was. It begins in the classroom when the Inspector demands that all of the pupils maintain "the same severe and uniform countenance."[62] Then comes "the sole prerequisite for a truly modern world: it's a single type of worker, the same countenance, the same clothes, the same gestures and words for each worker. In that way alone may the leader succeed in believing that a single human being is toiling and sweating."[63] And finally:

"A universal banality and insensitivity are spreading over everything."[64]

Full Powers. Did he ever exercise a single one of them himself, beyond those of the imagination? The position which gave him the most visibility was that of Goebbels's counterpart as Commissioner General of Information, a position created by Daladier at the onset of the "phoney war." In fact, he oversaw a staff of draft dodgers, misguided intellectuals, and military men who took orders from no one but the military. On the very day of his appointment, he was divested of his power over the press, over censorship, cinema, foreign relations, broadcasting, and special services. "I have to limit myself to giving little speeches, and those, only when I am given permission." He had the outward trappings of power: he *was* the appearance of power. It always had been that way for him.

He was a military officer for twenty-one days: promoted to temporary second lieutenant on 1 June 1915, he was wounded on the twenty-first of the same month and evacuated to face a future of hospitals, convalescences, vague assignments and missions to foreign lands, wearing his stripes but having no troops.

He was a civil servant for thirty-one years, but what power did he have? The administration of French schools abroad, the press bureau, the inspection of diplomatic and consular posts, all of which today have the scope of a major administrative unit or even a ministry, consisted at the time he headed them of scarcely more than a deputy and a couple of typists. The deputy—whether it was Paul Morand, Pierre Bressy, or Marcel Job—would be a friend, a young acquaintance, a partner, or a double—anything but a subordinate. The Chief set an example of being casual, and he was for a long time placed on the back burner, overseeing outmoded departments such as the Commission of Allied War Damages in Turkey.

He was never a diplomat, that is if a diplomat is defined as a plenipotentiary charged with representing his country, or even an embassy secretary charged with drafting an informational memo to the government. Did he dream about heading an embassy, which would in the normal run have been a reward for his assignment in Information? According to Morand, the Vichy government offered him the one in Athens, which he was said to decline.

He was never a property owner. He had visions of buying

a house in the country, but the project never materialized. He dreamed of a house in Touraine three months before his death: "What I need is the Loire."[65]

He certainly had the power that courage confers, but opportunities to display it are rare in times of peace: he had the courage to resist the terrible Bunau-Varilla, who had taken him on as secretary and asked him to write accommodating articles.[66] He had the courage to confront the formidable Poincaré, whose economic policies were undermining French instruction abroad. As head of French schools abroad, Giraudoux appealed to the public against his minister. Giraudoux lost his post as a result, but the French teachers abroad were saved.[67] And he had the courage to confront Goebbels, since it would have been easier to say, like Gide: "I definitely will not speak on the radio."[68]

As for the power of money, yes, he did possess that. And yet . . . he did not wait for a comfortable salary or for his substantial author's royalties to start dressing elegantly (see the recollections of Morand) or to collect the sketches of Poussin (see the beginning of *Siegfried and the Limousin*). Money gave him an easy life: attractive surroundings, the chance to give gifts—still, nothing extravagant or sumptuous.[69] If Jean Giraudoux shared the lifestyle of the well-to-do middle class, he never had the power attached to it: investments bringing in profits, extensive property holdings, the right to give orders, power over other people.

However, he witnessed from close quarters, and continuously, those powers that he did not have. He counted among his closest friends the aforementioned Abreu family (which owned a part of Havana and a mansion in the Saint-Germain district) and also Charles de Polignac (whose very name is a symbol). The little lieutenant frequently visited his staff officers; the junior diplomat imagined that he was wielding pencil and eraser at Versailles for the signing of treaties—something that was not entirely beyond the realm of possibility.[70] Edouard Herriot, minister of Foreign Affairs in 1932, named him to his cabinet. The Popular Front bestowed on him the ribbon of Commander of the Legion of Honor, and offered him the directorship of the Comédie française, which he refused. Finally, Daladier. . . .

His complete political writings have yet to be collected and studied in their historical context along with their conclusions and the purpose they served; for example, the opposition of France and the French people, to which he returned so often, implies at times the superiority of the idea of France over the

actual French people, at other times a denunciation of the substitution of a symbol for the living reality.[71] It is possible that
here, as elsewhere, Giraudoux's thought will appear to be
changeable and ambivalent, elusive and all the more dynamic
as a result. But it is possible also that political power will be
exposed as a special case, and an unproductive one, of a series
of powers in the plural, all of which are summed up for Giraudoux in the power of the written word, the only power that
he mastered, but this one fully.

Giraudoux's view on power must then be sought in the en-
tirety of his writings, and not only because it refers to the power
of engineers in the style of Jules Verne, such as the Dumas
that was mentioned in the beginning of *Siegfried and the
Limousin;*[72] that of landscape architects like Jean Forestier; ad-
venturers of the real world, scientists, explorers, diplomats, it
hardly matters as long as they are inventors and creators, practic-
ing like the Dubardeau brothers the synthesis of bodies and
the synthesis of nations. To a greater extent than an engineer
of souls (engineer = genius + ingenuity, says Michel Tournier),
and to a greater extent than an architect ("The engineer and
the architect are the two novelists of the globe," according to
Full Powers),[73] the writer has the power of a set designer who
weds the country to the countryside, *urbanisme* [city planning]
to urbanity, the nation to what is natural. "How consoling life
was going to be, if the real world could thus be sewn to an
imaginary world"![74]

CONCLUSION

"In the truly significant moments, other human beings are hardly more than parts of our own concert."[1] Did this egotist ever make a distinction between others and himself? Paul Morand rather naively points out that there are no quotations from other writers in Giraudoux's books.[2] Not a single epigraph, even in his eulogies, and not a single alexandrine line in his study of Racine. In truth, Giraudoux's work is full of quotations, but without the quotation marks. Scholars will never finish uncovering all the pastiches, allusions, parodies, and textual quotations. "What is the point of these debates? . . . Are there any quotation marks around the particles of your friend's body . . . which are perhaps already absorbed in the body of a beautiful child or a young lime tree"?[3] Giraudoux did not place quotation marks around quotations, nor around experiences, readings, the dreams of his friends or those of his schoolmasters and mistresses, nor around his very own.

He made his honey from others as well as from himself. His work is full of autobiographical details, and yet he wrote no autobiography.[4] When Sartre asked him to talk about himself, he began to write *Recollection From Two Existences*.[5] This was undoubtedly one existence too many for Sartre's liking. In Giraudoux's estimation, two existences were very little. What was the second of the two? Because the work is incomplete, we cannot know if it was to consist only of an ebb and flow of the past and present, some *Personal Recollections* inserted into a *Journal of the Bleak Years*. Did he not wish to reveal another life, woven of dreams, games, childishness, fantasies, and adventures—a fantastic existence of which our day-to-day life would at best be a shadow? He could have been the court recorder of his own existence, or put on a mask and proceeded to recreate his existence in new *Memories From Beyond the Grave*.* He preferred to come to us *non-larvatus* "with a totally

---

*Translator's Note: The three allusions refer to specific titles of French authors: *Mémoires intérieurs (Personal Recollections)* by François Mauriac, *Journal des*

unknown face, which looked like happiness,"[6] "as empty and devoid of a past as Adam was in the earthly paradise,"[7] or "Bergson on the right and a hardware merchant on the left."[8] Hiding the fact that he had nothing to hide, parading before the public "the age of fiancés, ravishers, and the exact age of the wind,"[9] rewriting and reworking toward a decrease in precision, he showed himself as adept at "suppressing his existence,"[10] as a child escaped from reform school. Protected from the risks of biography, he forged himself "a creature that was complete and finished, having its own rhythm and its own direction."[11]

Philippe Soupault wrote in 1923: "Jean Giraudoux did not need a life; I once knew where he was born and where he lived, but I have forgotten. Why try to remember what is useless? With his pen, he sketches his horoscope; he spins his memories and designs his projects."[12] Not content with "confiding in language,"[13] having understood that "the destiny of humanity is not to be found in the spoken word,"[14] he revealed himself in silence and in action, less intent however on leaving masterpieces and living his life, than on leaving an image of himself which would in turn inspire, stimulate thought and renew life: "We do not have a life; what are fifty or eighty years on the earth? But each one of us can exist if he has an existence that is legendary. The man or the woman who is not legendary is nothing. More than anything else, one must find one's legend."[15]

* * * * * * * * * * * *

Many thanks are extended to all the friends of Jean Giraudoux who assisted me and encouraged me. A special acknowledgment goes to Mr. Jean-Pierre Giraudoux, who has always generously welcomed the researchers and admirers of his father.

---

années noires (Journal of the Bleak Years) by Jean Guéhenno, and Mémoires d'outre-tombe (Memories From Beyond the Grave) by Chateaubriand.

NOTES

Translator's Note: All of the notes refer to the original texts cited by Professor Body. The English translations of the titles are given in parentheses or brackets and, where appropriate, the accepted English language title has been selected, such as Christopher Fry's translation of *La guerre de Troie n'aura pas lieu* (*Tiger at the Gates*) and Elizabeth Sergeant's translation of *Lectures pour une ombre* (*Campaigns and Intervals*). Titles of journals have not been translated in these notes. All references to plays are taken from *Théâtre complet* (Complete Theater) (Paris: Gallimard, 1982)—the Pléiade edition.

Preface

1. "All genres are combined in the modern theatre" (*Siegfried* 1.8, p. 22). On Giraudoux's theater, I refer the reader to Jacques Robichez, *Le théâtre de Giraudoux* (Société d'édition d'enseignement supérieur); and also Brett Dawson's thesis, *Giraudoux théoricien du théâtre*, University of Paris-Sorbonne, 1977, a mine of scholarly information as yet, alas, unpublished.

2. *Provinciales* (Provincial ways), pp. 9, 146, 105; *Souvenir de deux existences* (Recollection from two existences), p. 89. Gide wrote a review of *Provinciales* in the *Nouvelle Revue française* (June 1909). Text republished in *Nouveaux Prétextes* (New pretexts).

3. "Nuit à Châteauroux" (Night in Châteauroux) was published in the *Nouvelle Revue française* in 1919, and subsequently collected with other war stories in *Adorable Clio*, p. 81. On the relationship between Proust and Giraudoux, cf. J. B., "Sur deux chroniques oubliées" (On two forgotten chronicles), *Studi francesi* (July–September 1967).

4. *Simon le Pathétique* (Simon the pathetic), p. 87. See the *Cahiers Jean Giraudoux*, ed. Brett Dawson, no. 2–3 (1974) for a letter from Valéry to Giraudoux. Valéry describes Giraudoux's art very well, using concepts that were dear to him: modulation, substitution, transformation.

5. *Elpénor*, p. 134.

6. *Suzanne et le Pacifique* (Suzanne and the Pacific), p. 74. Michel Tournier expressed his admiration in *Le Monde*, 8 October 1982 ("Une île deserte signée Christian Bérard" [A desert island signed Christian Bérard]), and Marie-Jeanne Durry on the first page of her short study "L'univers de Giraudoux," *Mercure de France* (1961).

7. *Siegfried* 4.3, p. 68. On the occasion of Giraudoux's centennial, Jean Anouilh wrote to the organizers of the event: "I owe a great deal to Giraudoux. I was eighteen years old at the time of *Siegfried* and what I learned from it, on the three evenings I saw the play—I still know it almost by heart, with the exact inflection of each actor—was crucial for me."

8. *Ondine* 1.5, p. 772.

9. *Amphitryon 38* 1.3, p. 130.

10. *Sodome et Gomorrhe* (Sodom and Gomorrah) 1.2, p. 873.

11. Published in a small volume in a limited edition (Kra, 1928), "La Grande Bourgeoise" (The upper-class woman) was republished in the *Oeuvres littéraires diverses.*

12. *L'Ecole des Indifférents* (School for the indifferent), pp. 73–74.

13. Aragon, "Giraudoux et l'Achéron," *Confluences* (1944): 116, 120; special issue "Hommage à Giraudoux."

Chapter 1. The Author-Character

1. Y. Gandon, "Soliloque de J. G." (Soliloquy of J. G.), *Les Nouvelles littéraires*, 17 August 1929.

2. See particularly *Siegfried*, first conceived for the commercial theater, and *Amphitryon 38*, seen by its author as made "for the general public" (*Lettres*, [Klincksieck: Publications of the Sorbonne, 1975], p. 218).

3. E. Ripert, "Les débuts de J. Giraudoux" (The early works of J. Giraudoux), *Notre Combat*, 24 November 1939. See also Paul Morand, *Giraudoux. Souvenirs de notre jeunesse* (Giraudoux: Memories of our youth) (Geneva: La Palatine, 1948), p. 31.

4. Lucie Heymann, hired to teach during the Occupation, had clipped from *Le Petit Chambérien* a reproduction of Vuillard's picture and had placed it on the wall to show her pupils the correct way to sit when writing.

5. Fr. Lefèvre, *Une heure avec . . . Jean Giraudoux* (An hour with . . . Jean Giraudoux), first series, NRF (1924), and collected in *Cahiers*, no. 14.

6. *Annales*, 1 January 1929.

7. For details, see the Pléiade edition, pp. 1158–85, and especially p. 1166.

8. *Adorable Clio*, p. 125.

9. Ibid.

10. *Simon*, chap. 1, p. 21.

11. Philippe Soupault told me that he saw someone introduce himself to Suzanne Giraudoux after the death of her husband: "You do not know me, Madame, but I knew your husband very well; we had breakfast together for years, around 192–. —Quite impossible, sir. My husband used to have breakfast at home." They were both right: after leaving the house, Giraudoux would pay a visit to the Deux Magots.

12. *Electre* (Electra) 1.2, p. 605.

13. Chris Marker recounts the legend that credits him with a time that is highly improbable (50 seconds). Pierre Charreton could not find a single trace of this championship. The organization of university sports was at the time in its infancy. Other writers (*Arts et sports* [Limoges, 1956], and G. Prouteau, second *Anthologie des textes sportifs*, p. 49) suggest that he was champion of the French *military* (note conveyed by Charreton).

14. Reprinted in *Cahiers*, no. 6. See also no. 12.

15. *Simon*, p. 31.

16. *Littérature*, pp. 224, 215, 225.

17. Lefèvre, *Une heure avec . . .* (An hour with . . .), vol. 4 (1927), and *Cahiers*, no. 14.

18. The sources for the pages on Bernard Grasset are, on the one hand, the book of Gabriel Boillat, *La Librairie Bernard Grasset et les Lettres françaises* (The publishing house of Bernard Grasset and French letters) (Champion,

1974) and, on the other hand, a series of archival documents collected by Brett Dawson.

19. The sales figure did not exceed 80 copies by January 1910—330 copies by 30 September 1912.

20. I owe all this information also to Gabriel Boillat and to his article, "Comment on fabrique un succès: *Maria Chapdelaine*, (The making of a success: *Maria Chapdelaine*), Revue d'Histoire littéraire de la France* (March–April 1974).

21. See Brett Dawson's article: "De Harvard au Quai d'Orsay. Les débuts de Jean Giraudoux" (From Harvard to the Quai d'Orsay: The early works of Jean Giraudoux) in the special issue, "Jean Giraudoux," *Revue d'Histoire littéraire de la France* (1983).

22. Fr. Lefèvre, *Les Nouvelles littéraires*, 20 February 1926. *Cahiers*, no. 14.

23. *Le Côté de Guermantes* (The Guermantes Way) (Pléiade), pp. 326–27. See also A. Pizzorusso, *Tre Studi su Giraudoux* (Three studies of Giraudoux), p. 65, and J. Y. Tadié, *Revue d'Histoire littéraire de la France* (January–March, 1967).

24. Published in the *Nouvelle Revue française* of 1 June 1909, and reprinted in *Nouveaux Prétextes*.

25. *Hommage à J. Giraudoux*, Lycée of Châteauroux, p. 20.

26. See Dawson, "De Harvard au Quai d'Orsay."

27. *Simon*, p. 126.

Chapter 2. The Limousin Utopia

1. "Echo," one of the "Trois Fragments" (Three fragments) published in the journal *Athéna* (January 1906) and all signed by Jean-Emmanuel Manière, appeared as an appendix to *Provinciales* (Provincial ways) in the Emile-Paul edition (1927) and was reprinted thanks to Laurent Le Sage in *Modern Language Notes*, vol. 70 (April 1955), p. 289.

2. "Visite chez le Prince" (Visit to the prince), *La France sentimentale* (Sentimental France), p. 74.

3. *Les Cinq Tentations de La Fontaine* (The five temptations of La Fontaine), p. 13.

4. See the notes on *Judith* by Guy Teissier in the Pléiade edition, pp. 1320 and 1322, as well as my *Giraudoux et l'Allemagne* (Giraudoux and Germany), p. 329.

5. "Message à la Légion" (Message to the Legion), *Patrie* (Algeria), year 1, no. 3 (September 1941), 19–21. Excerpts have been published in *Voici la France de ce mois* (October 1941). It should be noted that this was the "French Legion of Fighters" the Pétain organization created immediately after the collapse of France, and not the "Legion of French Volunteers against Bolchevism," a gross error that occasionally has been made.

6. *Pleins Pouvoirs* (Full powers), p. 69. Michel Moreau has noted that Lower-Marche is part of Upper-Limousin and Upper-Quercy part of Lower-Limousin, so that it is necessary to transpose Upper and Lower! See *Giraudoux et le Limousin* (Giraudoux and the Limousin), Bellac (1982).

7. Response to the survey in the journal *Littérature*, no. 10 (December 1919): 22. See also chap. 3, p. 48.

8. *Siegfried et le Limousin*, p. 295.

9. See Moreau's text, *Giraudoux et le Limousin* (Giraudoux and the Limousin), p. 8. One may also refer to this publication of the Bellac Festival and the Jean Giraudoux Cultural Center to enjoy the counterpointing of quotations and iconography (60 documents and photographs, unfortunately reduced in size).

10. *Provinciales* (Provincial ways), p. 159 ("Allégories" 3: "A l'amour, à l'amitié" [To love, to friendship]).

11. *Littérature*, p. 286.

12. *Elpénor*, p. 64 ("Les Sirènes" [The sirens]).

13. "Visite chez le Prince" (Visit to the prince), *La France sentimentale* (Sentimental France), pp. 68–71; the report from *Feuillets d'Art*, 15 October 1919, "De Saint-Amand en Bourbonnais," (From Saint-Amand in Bourbonnais) was republished in *Or dans la nuit* (Gold in the night), pp. 100–108; *Siegfried et le Limousin*, pp. 47–49.

14. The Bruère monument (7 kilometers from Saint-Amand) is described in *Lectures pour une ombre (Campaigns and Intervals)*, p. 52, and mentioned on p. 100 in *Or dans la nuit* (Gold in the night), and on p. 48 in *Siegfried et le Limousin*.

15. "Charles-Louis Philippe," *Nouvelle Revue française*, 1 October 1937, was republished, with revisions, in *Littérature*, p. 177.

16. *Siegfried et le Limousin*, pp. 153–54.

17. Ibid., pp. 291–97.

18. "In beautiful adventures, the ending always brings you back to the country of departure" (*Pour Lucrèce* [For Lucrece] 2.5, p. 1090).

19. *Littérature*, p. 286.

20. *Lectures pour une ombre (Campaigns and Intervals)*, p. 140.

21. Letter of 20 September 1903, *Lettres*, p. 14.

22. *Siegfried et le Limousin*, p. 292.

23. *Simon*, p. 38.

24. Ibid., p. 36.

25. Letter to the director of the Ecole Normale Supérieure (Ernest Lavisse), Munich, early December 1905, *Lettres*, p. 94.

26. Letter of 11 August 1906, *Lettres*, p. 61.

27. Letter of 14 November 1937, *Lettres*, p. 251.

28. Letter to Louis Jouvet of 13 November 1936, "Correspondance entre Jean Giraudoux et Louis Jouvet" (Correspondence between Jean Giraudoux and Louis Jouvet), *Cahiers*, no. 9 (Grasset, 1980), p. 71.

29. Preface to the new edition of *Amica America* (1918) (Grasset, 1938), p. 10.

30. *Suzanne*, pp. 66–67. See Gérard Genette, *Palimpsestes. La littérature au second degré* (Palimpsests: Second-degree narrative) (du Seuil, 1982), p. 347.

31. *Littérature*, p. 250.

32. *Simon*, p. 112.

33. Variant of the *Fin de Siegfried* (End of Siegfried), *Théâtre complet* (Pléiade) p. 1270.

34. See Jacques Body, *Giraudoux et l'Allemagne* (Giraudoux and Germany), pp. 293–95.

35. *Siegfried* 3.5, p. 58.

36. An early draft manuscript. See *Intermezzo* (édition critique) by Colette Weil, publication of the University of Strasbourg (Ophrys Edition, 1975), p. 30.

37. *Amica America*, p. 215.

Chapter 3. The Eternal First

1. *Simon*, p. 8.

2. Ibid., p. 99.

3. Chris Marker, *Giraudoux par lui-même* (Giraudoux by himself), p. 5.

4. I am using information based solely on the account told to me by Philippe Soupault.

5. This curious text was established at the request of Adrienne Monnier, *Catalogue* no. 11 of Librairie Loliée, 72, rue de Seine.

6. B. Crémieux, *La Revue historique* (3 February 1923): 97. In this year, Giraudoux's candidate as a member of the panel of judges for the "Prize of the New World," was Soupault, whom he wanted to be appointed to the Quai d'Orsay. See also *Lettres*, p. 224.

7. Archives of the lycée of Châteauroux.

8. *Siegfried et le Limousin*, p. 182. The mention of Ecueillé, several lines farther on calls for comment: first in the canton, Pellevoisin being part of the canton of Ecueillé (Indre).

9. Giraudoux's honors, as a student of the lycée of Châteauroux and of the lycée Lakanal, as well as the results of his examination at the Ecole Normale Supérieure can be found in René Marill Albérès, *Esthétique et morale chez Jean Giraudoux* (Aesthetics and morality in the work of Jean Giraudoux) (Nizet, 1957), pp. 37 and 489–90 (appendix A). However, one should disregard the findings concerning his program for the *licence* (appendix C). One also may refer to my *Giraudoux et l'Allemagne* (Giraudoux and Germany), pp. 34 and 461–62 (appendix 2); similarly for details on the dissertation for the diploma and the *agrégation*, see pp. 89–107.

10. R. de Beauplan, "Les débuts littéraires de J. Giraudoux," (The early literature of J. Giraudoux), *Aspects* (3 March 1944). There actually existed an end-of-the-year ranking by subject. See R. Rolland, *Le cloître de la rue d'Ulm* (The cloister on the rue d'Ulm), pp. 250–51. Even supposing that this ranking continued through 1907—without leaving a bit of evidence in the archives—it could only have been beneficial to Giraudoux to the extent that he was, in his class, the only student of German.

11. *Simon*, p. 27.

12. One may judge it particularly from the letter that he sent from Munich to Ernest Lavisse, director of the Ecole Normale Supérieure, *Lettres*, p. 94.

13. See the account of his military record in Body, *Giraudoux et l'Allemagne* (Giraudoux and Germany), pp. 459–60.

14. Such examinations were organized in all departments of civil service, to make up for the massive loss of manpower in the Great War. Claudel was unkind when he used the term "gate-crashing" (*Candide*, 9 February 1944). On the good and bad relations of Giraudoux with Claudel, see my article "Sur deux chroniques oubliées" (On two forgotten chronicles), *Studi francesi* (September–December 1967) and the article of Michel Autrand, "Claudel et Giraudoux," *Revue d'Histoire littéraire de la France* (September–December 1983).

On Giraudoux's failure of 1909 and the examination of 1910, see Body, *Giraudoux et l'Allemagne* (Giraudoux and Germany), pp. 109–18, as well as *Cahiers*, no. 13 (1984): "Giraudoux et la diplomatie" (Giraudoux and diplomacy).

15. Interview by A. Warnod concerning *Electre (Electra)*, *Le Figaro* (11 May 1937).

16. *Choix des Elues* (Choice of the Elect), p. 32.

17. *Je suis partout* (I am everywhere) (4 February 1944).

18. *Simon*, p. 35.

19. The professor was named Francisque Vial. The story has been confirmed in Camille Martin's "Souvenirs de Khâgne: à Lakanal en 1902" (Recollections of Khâgne: At Lakanal in 1902) in *Le Figaro littéraire*, 11 February 1950 and by Alexandre Guinle, in Paul Guth and Maurice Toesca, "Potaches et Labadens" (Schoolboys and old buddies), *La Table Ronde* (1957).

20. Etienne Brunet, *Le Vocabulaire de J. Giraudoux* (Slatkine, 1978). On the phoney technical terms, see, for example, the final page of *Elpénor*, those "maritime operations that the translators cannot refrain from explaining, for the sake of the reader, in their own technical terms: he argued that there was a *conasse* (an 'imbecile') in the *virempot* ('virilpot'), then, the *masure* ('masture') having *soupié* ('supined'), he *bordina* ('puddied') the *astifin* ('astifine'): he was saved!" See also *La guerre de Troie n'aura pas lieu (Tiger at the Gates)*, "on not the *ramat* ('ramrod') but on the *écoutière* ('acutier')," 1.10, p. 511 and n. 1, or "the sail was *franc grosse* ('truly gross')," 2.12, p. 540 and n. 3.

On styles of language, and for the benefit of those who claim that all of Giraudoux's characters speak all the time like cabinet attachés, these responses at the beginning and end of a scene (1.4) from *La guerre de Troie n'aura pas lieu (Tiger at the Gates)*, p. 490 and p. 494):

> "Congratulations, Paris, You have been very busy in our absence."
> "Pretty busy. Thank you. . . ."
> "That was a fine thing you brought off that day!"
> "Must you play the older brother!"

21. Jean Cocteau, *Souvenir de Jean Giraudoux* (Memory of Jean Giraudoux) (Paris: Jacques Haumont, 1946), p. 19.

22. *Simon*, p. 32.

23. Philippe Berthelot, secretary general of the Quai d'Orsay, patron and friend of Jean Giraudoux, was the son of Marcelin Berthelot, the celebrated chemist and politician. On the relationship of Jean Giraudoux with Philippe Berthelot, one may consult their correspondence, edited by Brett Dawson in *Cahiers*, no. 13 (1984).

24. *Suzanne*, p. 31; *Or dans la nuit* (Gold in the night), p. 17.

25. *Littérature*, p. 20.

26. *Ibid.*, p. 211.

27. *Or dans la nuit* (Gold in the night), p. 31. In the same volume, one will find the *Hommage à Marivaux* (1943).

28. *Suzanne*, p. 133.

29. *Or dans la nuit* (Gold in the night), p. 32.

30. Lefèvre, "Une heure avec" (An hour with), *Nouvelles littéraires* (20 February 1926). *Cahiers*, no. 14.

31. *Simon*, p. 26. See J. Cl. Sertelon, *Giraudoux et le Moyen Age* (Giraudoux and the Middle Ages) (La Pensée Universelle, 1974), which I have both summarized and discussed: "Réception du Moyen Age et pastiche moyenâgeux dans l'oeuvre de Giraudoux" (The use of the Middle Ages and medieval pastiche in the work of Giraudoux), *La Licorne*, vol. 2, no. 6 (Faculty of Letters of Poitiers, 1982), pp. 265–83.

32. Lefèvre, "Une heure avec . . ." (An hour with . . .), *Les Nouvelles littéraires* (20 February 1926).

33. *Simon*, p. 21.

34. *Lettres*, p. 94.

35. See Body, *Giraudoux et l'Allemagne* (Giraudoux and Germany), p. 61: "La vie à Munich" (Life in Munich).

36. See *Lettres*, p. 83, and *Siegfried et le Limousin*, p. 205.

37. *La Française et la France* (The Frenchwoman and France) (Gallimard, 1951), p. 88.

38. *Lettres*, p. 156.

39. Lefèvre, "Une heure avec . . ." (An hour with . . .), *Les Nouvelles littéraires* (20 February 1926).

40. *Souvenir de deux existences* (Recollection from two existences), p. 36.

41. *Electre*, "Lamento" (The Gardener's lament), p. 642.

42. "Divertissement de Siegfried" (Divertimento of Siegfried), variant A of p. 83, p. 1262.

43. *Simon*, p. 54.

44. See Albérès, *Esthétique et morale* (Aesthetics and morality), p. 76.

45. In fact, Herriot was summoning to his service the scholar and writer, who had been overlooked for six years in a low-ranking service, the Commission of Allied War Damages in Turkey. Giraudoux showed himself as "the most detached of attachés," in the words of Herriot himself, who nevertheless made a point of honoring him by presiding over the ceremonies organized in Bellac in 1951, with the participation of Louis Jouvet and his troupe. See E. Herriot, *Jean Giraudoux* (de la Passerelle, 1951), p. 55.

46. *Simon*, p. 55.

47. See *Lettres*, p. 55.

48. Simone Ratel, "Entretiens avec Jean Giraudoux . . ." (Conversations with Jean Giraudoux), *Comoedia* (18 June 1928), republished in *Dialogues à une seule voix* (Dialogue with a single voice); see *Cahiers*, no. 14.

49. "Le théâtre contemporain en Allemagne et en France" (The contemporary theater in Germany and France), *Conférencia* (5 December 1931), republished in *Or dans la nuit* (Gold in the night), p. 132.

50. *Siegfried* 1.6, p. 16.

51. Genette, *Palimpsestes*.

52. On this subject, see Jacques Robichez's paper in the *Cahiers de l'Association internationale des Etudes françaises* (Paris, 1982) and chapter 2 of his *Théâtre de Giraudoux* (Société d'édition d'enseignement supérieur, 1976). On p. 65, there is a particularly amusing example: the way in which the natives of *Supplément au voyage de Cook* (Supplement to Cook's voyage), at the beginning of scene 3, recite as a chorus four lines of Vigny (*La Colère de Samson* [Samson's anger]):

The Wife. Man always needs caressing and loving.
The Young Aunt. His mother showers him with love when he enters life.

Outourou. And her arm is the first to calm him and rock him.
The Daughter. And gives him a desire for love and indolence.

53. Homer being in a class of his own since, to use once gain the terminology of Gérard Genette, he has both the status of *hypotexte* and that of *hypertexte*.
54. *Choix des Elues* (Choice of the elect), p. 155.
55.. Simon, p. 28.
56. Ibid.
57. *Amphitryon 38*, p. 82.
58. Robichez, *Le théâtre de Giraudoux*, p. 183.
59. "Prière sur la tour Eiffel" (Prayer on the Eiffel tower), *Juliette au pays des hommes* (Juliette in the land of men), pp. 143–44.
60. *Simon*, pp. 20–21.
61. *Intermezzo* 1.6, p. 296.
62. Etienne Brunet, *Le Vocabulaire de J. Giraudoux*, pp. 549–51.
63. *Simon*, p. 59.
64. *Ondine* 2.1, p. 795.
65. "Sur la caricature" (Concerning caricature), *Les Nouvelles littéraires*, 5 November 1932. Text republished in *Littérature*, with several variants, under the title, "Caricature et satire," p. 187.

Chapter 4. The Player

1. Maurice Martin du Gard, *Les Mémorables* (Memorabilia), vol. 3 (Grasset, 1978), p. 285.
2. *Bella*, pp. 11–12. Cf. also "La Grande Bourgeoise" (The upper-class woman), pp. 272–73.

. . . he began to play cards with three regulars; first manille, then piquet, and—the game becoming more sophisticated as the players got to know each other—they ended up playing bridge.
"I bet that you know the names and ages of their wives," asked Françoise. . . .
"There were three of them," replied Durlan. "The stage manager from Lumignac, who took part in the Marchand mission, the first man ever to play poker in Ouaddai. They were missing the eight of spades. They had to go all the way to Abyssinia to find one."

3. *Visitations*, pp. 93–94.
4. This photograph is reproduced in the volume *Lettres*, which contains a chapter on the family in Toulouse, p. 109.
5. *Visitations*, p. 96.
6. See especially *Pour Lucrèce* (For Lucrece) 2.5, p. 1089: "Intermission in the drama, Lucile. Here is where bourgeois comedy will reclaim its rights."
7. Morand, *Souvenirs de notre jeunesse* (Memories of our youth), p. 19 (teasing); p. 19 (hundred meters); p. 47 (decorations).
8. Told to the author by his deputy, Pierre Bressy.
9. André Beucler, "Giraudoux mystificateur et Jouvet spectateur" (Giraudoux the prankster and Jouvet the spectator), *Revue des Deux Mondes* (15 June 1957).

10. Beucler, *Les instants de Giraudoux* (The instants of Giraudoux), p. 147. See also, pp. 137–39 concerning the game of the dogs, with Giraudoux "reverting to childhood."

11. Told to the author by André Beucler.

12. "Le problème de la France se pose ainsi" (France's problem may be put this way), from seven unpublished pages stored in the Jacques Doucet collection in the Bibliothèque Nationale.

13. *L'Epoque* (16 April 1947).

14. Maurice Bourdet, "Jean Giraudoux," *Nouvelle Revue critique* (1928), which is devoted to Giraudoux the novelist and appeared three months before the premiere of the play *Siegfried*. *Textes choisis* (Selected texts) by Jean Giraudoux, collected and introduced by René Lalou (Grasset, 1932). Marker, *Giraudoux par lui-même* (Giraudoux by himself). Albérès, *Esthétique et morale* (Aesthetics and morality).

15. *Or dans la nuit* (Gold in the night), p. 68.

16. Morand, *Souvenirs de notre jeunesse* (Memories of our youth), p. 142.

17. *Or dans la nuit* (Gold in the night), p. 64.

18. *Electre*, act 1, p. 600.

19. Marc Aucuy, *La jeunesse de Giraudoux* (Giraudoux's youth), p. 163.

20. "He was musical" (Morand, *Souvenirs de notre jeunesse* (Memories of our youth), p. 49.

21. Lefèvre, "Une heure avec . . ." (An hour with . . .), *Les Nouvelles littéraires* (20 February 1926). *Cahiers*, no. 14.

22. See the first act of *Siegfried*, notes to the Pléiade, p. 1149, n. 6.

23. *Fin de Siegfried* (End of Siegfried), p. 93.

24. Marie-Jeanne Durry, "L'univers de Giraudoux" (Giraudoux's universe), *Mercure de France* (1961); Charles Mauron, *Le théâtre de Giraudoux. Etude psychocritique* (Giraudoux's theater: Psychocritical study) (Corti, 1971).

25. Simon, p. 194.

26. *Judith* 3.4, p. 260.

27. *L'Apollon de Bellac* (The Apollo of Bellac), scene 9, p. 944.

28. Simon, p. 123.

29. Lefèvre, "Une heure avec . . ." (An hour with . . .), *Les Nouvelles littéraires* (2 June 1923), *Cahiers*, no. 14 (1985). Albérès, *Esthétique et morale* (Aesthetics and morality), especially p. 65 and p. 149.

30. "Nuit à Châteauroux" (Night in Châteauroux), *Adorable Clio*, p. 86.

31. Archives of the lycée of Châteauroux. One is reluctant to take certain details in *Simon* as autobiographical: "They never wrote to me," p. 18, and p. 30: "That was the period when the pictures on postage stamps changed every six months: some of those stamps my father never used, because he did not have the time."

32. Simon, p. 125.

33. Ibid., pp. 122–23.

34. Aucuy, *La jeunesse de Giraudoux* (Giraudoux's youth), pp. 20–21.

35. Simon, p. 194.

36. Lothar Knapp, *Der messianische Gedanke im Werk Jean Giraudoux'* (The messianic thinking in the work of Jean Giraudoux) (Heidelberg, 1964).

37. First draft of *Siegfried* (Pléiade), p. 1224.

38. Simon, p. 129 and p. 209.

39. Ibid., p. 189.

40. *La guerre de Troie n'aura pas lieu* (Tiger at the Gates) 1.6, p. 497.

41. *Simon*, p. 197. Giraudoux points out himself that his birthday falls on the day of Saint-Narcissus (*Lettres*, p. 133).

42. "Prière sur la tour Eiffel" (Prayer on the Eiffel tower), *Juliette*, p. 143.

43. *Simon*, p. 166.

44. *Aventures de Jérôme Bardini* (The adventures of Jerome Bardini), p. 236.

45. Ibid., p. 201.

46. *Simon*, p. 158.

47. *Elpénor*, p. 130.

48. *L'Ecole des Indifférents* (School for the indifferent), p. 110.

49. *Fin de Siegfried* (End of Siegfried), scene 2, p. 96.

50. *La France sentimentale* (Sentimental France), p. 183.

51. *Intermezzo* 3.4, p. 347.

52. *La guerre de Troie n'aura pas lieu (Tiger at the Gates)* 1.8, p. 506.

53. Mauron, *Le théâtre de Giraudoux*, p. 11.

54. *La France sentimentale* (Sentimental France), p. 188.

55. *Amica America*, p. 24.

56. *Intermezzo* 3.6, p. 355. The variants are: "Intoxication . . . Freudianism . . ." and "Superstition. Intoxication . . . Freudianism." In each case, the reply is placed in the mouth of the Inspector, which lessens its impact because the Inspector is generally the mouthpiece for falsehoods.

57. *Littérature*, p. 101. (*Freude* means joy in German.)

58. *Les Cinq Tentations* (The five temptations), pp. 61 and 91.

59. Letter to Morand cited by him in *Souvenirs de notre jeunesse* (Memories of our youth), p. 57.

60. One could almost write an essay on Giraudoux's "sluice gates." Defined in *Provinciales* (Provincial ways) on p. 31 as "a gentle force which places everything on the same level," they are the metaphor for smooth transitions (*L'Ecole des Indifférents* [School for the indifferent], pp. 195 and 228; *La France sentimentale* [Sentimental France], p. 73; *Or dans la nuit* [Gold in the night], p. 188); they are an indispensable part of quiet landscapes and happy dénouements (*Adorable Clio*, p. 213; *Siegfried et le Limousin*, p. 303); they are simultaneously symbols of art ("A poet, sluice gate of language," *Juliette*, pp. 141–42) and of wisdom (*Les Hommes-tigres* [The tiger men], p. 13), disguising the crises of existence—including death—under the harmless name of "lockage" (*Combat avec l'Ange* [Combat with the angel], p. 61). Benjamin Crémieux was right to suggest that Giraudoux defined himself through the character of the Druggist in *Intermezzo*, and to quote him as saying: "My presence always serves as a lock between two moments that are not on the same level, between happiness and misfortune, the precise and the confused, or vice-versa" ("L'anti-réalisme au théâtre" [Anti-realism in the theater], *Nouvelle Revue française*, 1 January 1933). This use of water imagery combines an ethic of equilibrium with an aesthetics of movement.

61. "Mirage de Bessines" (Mirage of Bessines), *La France sentimentale* (Sentimental France), p. 19.

62. *Annales*, December 1929.

63. Mauron, *Le théâtre de Giraudoux*, p. 10.

64. "Je présente Bellita" (I present Bellita), *La France sentimentale* (Sentimental France), p. 18.

65. Ibid., pp. 29–30.

66. *Juliette*, pp. 101, 118, 120, 122, 119, 115.

67. "Mirage," pp. 186–88.

68. *Les Cinq Tentations* (The five temptations), p. 91.

69. From the dog named Miraut who saved his life when he was a baby (Pléiade, p. 1214, and *Souvenir de deux existences* [Recollection from two existences], p. 12) to Puck, the big brown poodle and inseparable companion of his later years, and in between, the dog named Black from his youth (*Lettres*, pp. 53, 75), Giraudoux always had greater respect for animals than for humans, as did the Madwoman of Chaillot (final speech in the play, p. 1031). Note, in particular, in *Eglantine*, the relationship of Fontranges with his horses and his dogs, and his meeting with the stag; in *Siegfried* 3.5, p. 57, n. 1 and p. 58), the mission of "personifying France" being entrusted (much to the indignation of René Doumic) to a dog: "A poodle. He is white, and like all white dogs in France, he is called Black"; in *Electre*, the tirade of the hedgehogs (1.3, pp. 610–12); the tirade of the she-wolf (p. 614), and the tirade of the ducks (1.13, p. 639), and last but not least the Gardener's dog, "Entracte" (p. 641). Giraudoux's bestiary has yet to be studied, even after Hugues Plaideux's dissertation, *L'Animal dans l'oeuvre de J. G.* (Animals in the work of J. G.) (Maisons-Alfort, 1980); but the importance he assigns them is clearly indicated in "La bête et l'écrivain" (The animal and the writer), *Littérature*, p. 189, and in "Les animaux rappellent à l'homme d'aujourd'hui la vie naturelle" (Animals take modern man back to nature), *Oeuvres littéraires diverses*, p. 643.

70. It is even more difficult to assess the role of plants in Giraudoux's works, but at least two passages sum up what one might call the wisdom of plant life, one of which is at the beginning of his career ("Le dernier rêve d'Edmond About" [The final dream of Edmond About], *Contes d'un Matin* [Tales for a morning], p. 174): "I would have waited for her, calmly, immobile, and patient, like trees waiting for rain"; the other in a later text (*Visitations*, p. 84): "[Men] will no longer have wars when they agree to become planted, immobile, each one planted apart from the other, in clumps, in geometric formations, or in rows. . . ." In short, the ideal of *Intermezzo* 1.6: "The tree is the immobile brother of man."

71. "Jouvet. I am not talking about love of the theatre. I am talking about love. Love of people, animals, and plants. If this whole audience, with the lights dimmed, is now fused into one, communing with itself in the darkness, it is so as to lose itself, to give itself up, to surrender. It is risking its very self in the general emotion" (*L'Impromptu de Paris* [The Paris impromptu], scene 3, p. 704).

72. *Juliette*, chap. 6.

73. *Littérature*, p. 101.

74. *Littérature*, pp. 30, 36, 31.

75. *Jérôme Bardini*, p. 49. See also what Geneviève says in *Siegfried* 2.1, p. 26: "I have never been reduced as I am today to a corporeal being so impersonal and to a soul so diffuse. I feel all too well that the only chance I have to reach Forestier is through what is least individual and most tenuous in myself. I am mobilizing all of my general ideas and timeless feelings."

This theme of amnesia and depersonalization has been well discussed by Albérès, *Esthétique et morale* (Aesthetics and morality), pp. 260–61.

76. *Elpénor*, pp. 17, 34, 35.

77. *Siegfried* 2.2, p. 29.

78. *Or dans la nuit* (Gold in the night), p. 63.

79. *L'Impromptu de Paris* (The Paris impromptu), scene 1, p. 692.

Chapter 5. Feminine Singular

1. *L'Ecole des Indifférents* (School for the indifferent), p. 51.

2. "She who wishes to see our family gradually improve itself" (*L'Ecole des Indifférents*, p. 213).

3. See *Lettres*, and Morand, *Souvenirs de notre jeunesse* (Memories of our youth), p. 30.

4. *Lettres*, p. 53: "Does she sit down now during meals?"

5. Anne Lacoste died 4 November 1943; her son Jean, 31 January 1944.

6. See, for example, the tax collector-inspector in "Sainte Estelle," *Provinciales* (Provincial ways), pp. 54–56; the employee of the tollhouse in "Le Petit Duc" (The little duke), pp. 113 and 135; and the road surveyer in "La Pharmacienne" (The lady pharmacist), p. 224. See in particular the father of *Simon* in chap. 1, and p. 123, and also *Siegfried et le Limousin*, p. 292 and thereafter. See also *Souvenir de deux existences* (Recollection from two existences), p. 111.

7. Bernard the weakling imagines himself to be the son of an exiled prince. As for the one who passes for his father, see *L'Ecole des Indifférents* (School for the indifferent), pp. 190–91.

8. *Simon*, p. 125. I have not dealt with the fleeting, though eloquent, reference in *L'Ecole des Indifférents* (School for the indifferent), p. 191. Perhaps the mother-son relationship would have been developed in *Les Gracques* (The Gracchi). In any event, there is nothing autobiographical in the Clytemnestra-Orestes relationship!

9. *Supplément au Voyage de Cook* (Supplement to Cook's Voyage), scene 3, pp. 563–64. See also p. 191, note 52.

10. *Siegfried et le Limousin*, p. 301.

11. *L'Ecole des Indifférents* (School for the indifferent), p. 73. See also the fragment of *Siegfried*, p. 1228.

12. "Nuit à Châteauroux" (Night in Châteauroux), in *Adorable Clio*, p. 65.

13. See Clotilde Marsaudon and the little Bohemian girl in *Souvenir de deux existences* (Recollection from two existences), pp. 7 and 32.

14. Jean Giraudoux gave Marie Defoulenay the manuscript *La Rosière des Chamignoux* (The maiden of Chamignoux), in which she played a role along with Renée Lacoste (*Cahiers du Bourbonnais*, 2d quarter, [1972], p. 40).

15. *L'Apollon de Bellac* (The Apollo of Bellac), scene 2, p. 924.

16. *Les Cahiers bourbonnais*, 2d quarter, [1972], p. 43. Jeanne, later Mrs. Chamboux, often welcomed her cousin "in the rural setting of her small property in Corrèze, on a small hillside of Millevache," and he would write, in particular, the second act of *Ondine*, sitting next to the tiny pond, "all green with algae and water lilies" (Colette Weil, "Petite histoire d'un manuscrit. L'*Ondine* de Sornac" [The short history of a manuscript. The *Ondine* of Sornac], *Cahiers*, no. 2–3, p. 115).

17. It is possible to relate this illness to the typhoid mentioned in *Souvenir de deux existences* (Recollection from two existences), p. 12.

18. *Provinciales* (Provincial ways), p. 34. The bonds between brother and sister are developed in *Electre* 1.6 and 1.8—idealized to the point of nominalism: "O ungrateful sister who recognizes me only by name!"

19. *Premier Ecrits* (Early works), edited by C. Weil, will appear in the Pléiade. See also, in the chronicles of *Feuillets d'Art*, "De Saint-Amand en Bourbon-

nais" (From Saint-Amand in Bourbonnais) (*Or dans la nuit* [Gold in the night], p. 100), a certain allusion to "women factory workers in the jewel factory, seduced by Mr. Bloch in the nation's linen rooms."

20. "La Pharmacienne" (The lady pharmacist), *Provinciales* (Provincial ways), pp. 209 and 215.

21. See *Lettres*, p. 109, and p. 169: "Do you have a photograph of Anne-Marie; I would like to see it."

22. *Lettres*, pp. 118 and 119.

23. *L'Ecole des Indifférents* (School for the indifferent), p. 105.

24. *L'Ecole des Indifférents* (School for the indifferent), p. 109.

25. *Lettres*, p. 66. See also *Giraudoux et l'Allemagne* (Giraudoux and Germany), pp. 65–68.

26. *Siegfried et le Limousin* pp. 94–96.

27. We have one of these letters in the archives of Giraudoux's native home, as well as a photograph with the following inscription: "a nice little plump person. . . ."

28. *L'Ecole des Indifférents* (School for the indifferent), p. 132.

29. *Simon*, p. 63.

30. Hence the pseudonym Jean Cordelier used in *Contes d'un Matin* (Tales for a morning).

31. At that time, situated at 5, rue de l'Ecole-de-Medécine.

32. Reproduced in Morand, *Souvenirs de notre jeunesse* (Memories of our youth), p. 121.

33. See *Lettres*, pp. 231 to 244, and *Or dans la nuit* (Gold in the night), p. 75.

34. *Provinciales* (Provincial ways), p. 156.

35. *L'Ecole des Indifférents* (School for the indifferent), p. 77.

36. He saw Mrs. Adams again in Paris in 1910, and in 1915, he was still using a pen she gave him for the fun of making Suzanne jealous.

37. *L'Ecole des Indifférents* (School for the indifferent), p. 139.

38. *Jérôme Bardini*, p. 237. See also Morand, *Souvenirs de notre jeunesse* (Memories of our youth), p. 130: "His real mistresses were his teachers" and Giraudoux's essay on Racine, *Littérature*, p. 41: "It was with them [his heroines] that he had his true love affairs, from the time he first read about them."

39. *Simon*, pp. 26, 81, 30, 204.

40. See Albérès, *Esthétique et morale* (Aesthetics and morality), especially, pp. 133–40 and pp. 448–54.

41. *Simon*, pp. 65, 78, 88, and 89.

42. *Adorable Clio*, p. 65.

43. *Simon*, p. 99.

44. *Eglantine*, pp. 60 and 79.

45. *Provinciales* (Provincial ways), pp. 156, 157, and 163.

46. G. Guitard-Auviste, *Paul Morand* (Hachette, 1981), p. 131.

47. "Whenever an author described love, I would be so shocked that I would throw away the book" (*Simon*, p. 128).

48. *Judith* 2.8, p. 254.

49. *Judith* 2.2, p. 234.

50. *Simon*, p. 81.

51. *Lettres*, pp. 129 and 139.

52. *Lettres*, pp. 145 and 160.

53. Dawson, "De Harvard au Quai d'Orsay" (From Harvard to the Quai d'Orsay), p. 721.

54. Early draft of *Siegfried*, p. 1230.

55. Letters to his parents, 21 February 1909.

56. See Morand, *Souvenirs de notre jeunesse* (Memories of our youth), p. 41, and Dawson's article, "De Harvard au Quai d'Orsay."

57. Thanks are due to Claude and Jacques Abreu, who graciously forwarded these letters that their aunt had kept and organized, and Yann Martin, who transcribed them.

58. *Intermezzo* 3.3, p. 342.

59. See M. Barthélemy, "La Carrière de J. G." (The career of J. G.), *Cahiers*, no. 13 (1984), p. 17.

60. *Siegfried et le Limousin*, p. 20. The earlier description of the three Poussin sketches is accurate. Jean Giraudoux kept them until his death. Two of them are today the property of the museum in Rouen.

61. Letter of 10 May 1912.

62. Morand, *Souvenirs de notre jeunesse* (Memories of our youth), p. 43.

63. Ibid., p. 39.

64. *Simon*, p. 67.

65. Morand, *Souvenirs de notre jeunesse* (Memories of our youth), p. 135.

66. "Charles-Louis Philippe," *Littérature*, p. 115.

67. *L'Ecole des Indifférents* (School for the indifferent), p. 53.

68. *Simon*, p. 180.

69. Letter to Lilita, 29 May 1913.

70. Letter to Lilita, 21 March 1912.

71. *Lettres*, p. 175.

72. See Guy Teissier, "Portrait de Giraudoux en jeune(s) homme(s)" (A portrait of Giraudoux as a young man [as young men]), *Cahiers de l'Association international des Etudes françaises*, no. 34 (1982), p. 196. The order of the chapters would also be changed; see Albérès, *Esthétique et morale* (Aesthetics and morality) with the following correction: in the table on p. 258, switch "1923 edition" (in fact, 1926) and "1918 edition."

73. *Simon*, p. 180.

74. Preface to *Suzanne*, and *Or dans la nuit* (Gold in the night), pp. 84–90.

75. Early draft of *Siegfried*, pp. 1203–1204. See also *Adorable Clio*, p.218.

76. Morand, *Souvenirs de notre jeunesse* (Memories of our youth), pp. 118–19.

77. *Lettres*, p. 179.

78. *Lettres*, p. 183.

79. Henraux subsequently divorced her, and Lilita ended her days, following the Second World War (and thus after the death of Jean Giraudoux) a devotee of the Hindu religion.

80. See *Giraudoux et l'Allemagne* (Giraudoux and Germany), p. 269, and Barthélemy, "La Carrière de J. G." (The career of J. G.), *Cahiers*, no. 13 (1984), p. 21.

81. On the front page of *L'Eclair* (27 April 1923), Béraud accused Giraudoux of capitalizing on his position in the *service des oeuvres* to bring fame to a coterie of tiresome writers, who had neither talent nor success: André Gide, Paul Claudel, André Suarès, and Jules Romains, to name a few. Giraudoux answered in *Les Nouvelles littéraires* (2 June 1923) with all the diplomacy and firmness that were appropriate. *Cahiers*, no. 14, pp. 31–37.

82. Gonzague Truc, *La Grande Revue*, 1 March 1923.

83. "Whose right is it to detain you, if not the right of this house!" (*Sodome et Gomorrhe* 1.3, p. 877. See also *Choix des Elues* [Choice of the elect], p. 83).

84. *Sodome et Gomorrhe* 1.3, p. 877.

85. *Jérôme Bardini*, p. 63.

86. *Combat avec l'Ange* (Struggle with the angel), p. 30. Here we find the portrait of the governess, Amparo, p. 116, and that of her daughter, Baba, p. 117. In reality, they were not Spanish but Italian women. As for the horse which was purchased, with his friend Albert Duggan (Alberto, p. 206), and which won the Jockey Prize, he was not named Strip the Willow (p. 206), but . . . Puma.

I have attempted to explain this collection of allusions and concealed truths in my contribution to the *Mélanges Jacques Robichez: Cent ans de littérature française* (A medley of studies in honor of Jacques Robichez: One hundred years of French literature) (Société d'édition d'enseignement supérieur, 1987): "Jean Giraudoux et ses modèles feminins. Début de réflexion sur l'art du portrait à ressemblance évitée" (Jean Giraudoux and his female models: Preliminary thoughts on the art of the portrait avoiding real likeness).

Thanks are due to Anita F. de Madero, who was kind enough to impart to me all the information I have given here concerning her.

87. *Ondine* 3.5, p. 845.

88. *Electre* 2.9, p. 684.

89. *Combat avec l'Ange* (Struggle with the angel), p. 32.

90. Manuscript notation on a copy (dedicated to her husband and to him alone, which explains her rage) of Paul Morand, *Chronique du XXe siècle. Magie noire* (Twentieth century chronicle: Black magic) (Grasset, 1928), which Maurice Barthélemy came upon in the Giraudoux Library currently preserved in Bellac.

91. See the postscript to my contribution to the *Mélanges Jacques Robichez* and my article "Giraudoux vu par Sartre" (Giraudoux as viewed by Sartre), *Oeuvres et critiques*, 2, 1, *Prose romanesque du XXe siècle*, ed. J.-M. Place (1977), pp. 51–58.

92. All that follows concerning Isabelle has been drawn from Laurent Le Sage and Lucie Heymann, "Les dernières années de J. G." (The final years of Jean Giraudoux), *Cahiers*, no. 8 (1979), pp. 5–60.

93. Jean-Pierre Giraudoux, *Le Fils* (The son) (Grasset, 1967), pp. 100–101.

94. Giraudoux had already said the same thing to Anita, who, besides, had good reason to think that she had inspired "the true Isabelle," the one in *Intermezzo*. In any event, the saying itself had already appeared in *Ondine* 1.4, pp. 770–71.

95. Variant of *Siegfried*, p. 1249.

96. *Intermezzo*, early draft edited by Weil, p. 1435.

97. *Sodome et Gomorrhe* 2.7, p. 903.

98. At the time of the premiere in Rio, as well as the premiere in Paris (1947), the title was *L'Apollon de Marsac* (The Apollo of Marsac). The change of *Marsac* to *Bellac* appeared in the galley sheets of the edition published by Grasset, which Giraudoux had corrected prior to his death, and in a letter of spring 1942 (see the note of J. Delort in the Pléiade edition, p. 1706 and p. 1708, n. 1).

99. *La Folle de Chaillot* (*The Madwoman of Chaillot*), end of act 2, p. 1030.

100. *Le Sport* (Sports), a small volume published in the collection *Notes*

et *Maximes* (Hachette, 1928), has been reprinted in the *Cahiers*, no. 6 (1977), p. 36 in the latter edition.

101. *La Française et la France* (The Frenchwoman and France), p. 201.
102. *Or dans la nuit* (Gold in the night), p. 178.
103. *L'Ecole des Indifférents* (School for the indifferent), pp. 139–40.
104. *Tessa* 1.1.17, p. 388.
105. *L'Apollon de Bellac* (The Apollo of Bellac), scene 9, p. 943.
106. *Jérôme Bardini*, p. 63.
107. Ibid., p. 82.
108. *Cantique des cantiques* (Song of Songs), scene 4, p. 740.
109. *Ondine* 2.5 and 2.4, pp. 845 and 842.
110. *Supplément au Voyage de Cook* (Supplement to Cook's Voyage), scenes 3 and 9.
111. *Judith* 2.4, p. 245. Until 1982, every published edition included an error from the original: *voyageurs* (travelers) for *voyeurs*. . . .
112. *La guerre de Troie n'aura pas lieu* (Tiger at the Gates) 2.8, p. 531 and 1.8, p. 507.
113. Ibid., p. 531.
114. Ibid., p. 493.
115. *Cantique des cantiques* (Song of Songs), scene 8, p. 754.
116. *Siegfried et le Limousin*, p. 205.
117. *Ondine* 1.9, p. 788.
118. *Sodome et Gomorrhe* 2.7, p. 905.

Chapter 6. The Presence of One Now Absent

1. Gaston Imbault, "J. G. et Saint-Amand-Montrond" (J. G. and Saint-Amand-Montrond), *Les Cahiers Bourbonnais*, (Moulins, 1973), p. 10.
2. As told to me by Bressy.
3. See "Correspondance Giraudoux-Jouvet" (Correspondence of Giraudoux and Jouvet), *Cahiers*, no. 9 (1980), p. 106.
4. Beucler, *Les Instants de Giraudoux* (The instants of Giraudoux), pp. 29 and 26.
5. See *Siegfried et le Limousin* and the four chapters (part 2, book 3, chaps. 1–4) on this novel in Body, *Giraudoux et l'Allemagne* (Giraudoux and Germany).
6. Léon Moussinac, *L'Humanité*, 1 December 1935.
7. *Je suis partout* (I am everywhere), 15 October 1943. One may find in the same publication on the day following the burial of Jean Giraudoux: "Everybody who is anybody in Gaullist Paris gathered around the literary catafalque of the author of *Bella*."
8. *Jérôme Bardini*, p. 89.
9. Privas, July; *Or dans la nuit* (Gold in the night), pp. 221, 216, 220, 218. In fact, *Or dans la nuit* (1969) is not Giraudoux's title: this volume collected posthumously a certain number of texts of literary and art criticism, and numerous essays that Giraudoux had not included in *Littérature*. *Or dans la nuit* was nearly entitled *Littérature II*. In the bibliographical notes of that edition, I dated this text July 1941 or 1942. This was in error; it undoubtedly dates from July 1940.
10. *Electre* 1.4, p. 618.

11. *La Folle (The Madwoman)*, act 2, p. 995.

12. "La Grande Bourgeoise" (The upper-class woman), *Oeuvres littéraires diverses*, p. 279.

13. *Intermezzo* 1.4, pp. 283–84.

14. *Electre* 1.3, p. 609, and "Entracte," pp. 642–43.

15. *Jérôme Bardini*, p. 240.

16. *Eglantine*, p. 228.

17. *Electre* 1.3, p. 609.

18. "Nuit à Châteauroux" (Night in Châteauroux), *Adorable Clio*, p. 67.

19. *Amphitryon 38* 2.2, p. 837.

20. *Ondine* 3.4, p. 837.

21. *Intermezzo* 3.2, p. 336.

22. "L'Orgueil" (Pride) was published in his work entitled *Les Sept Péchés capitaux* (The seven capital sins) (Kra, 1929). It was published in the *Oeuvres littéraires diverses*, p. 628, and the *Cahiers*, no. 11.

23. Morand, *Souvenirs de notre jeunesse* (Memories of our youth), p. 25.

24. The "Discours sur le théâtre" (Discourse on theater) (1931) was included in *Littérature*. Giraudoux loved puns, but he was not amused when Gérard d'Houville (Madame Henri de Régnier), in her review of this play set in Behtulia, remarked that she was *"embéthulée"* (*Littérature*, p. 238). [**Translator's Note:** The verb *embêter* means to bother or to annoy, and the suffix *uler* conveys the sense of a diminutive in verb form.]
    Concerning *L'Impromptu de Paris* (The Paris impromptu), see Dawson's notes in the Pléiade edition.

25. *Simon*, p. 59.

26. See notes 69 and 70 in chap. 4 ("The Player").

27. *L'Apollon de Bellac (The Apollo of Bellac)*, scene 9, pp. 943–44.

28. Lefèvre, "Une heure avec . . ." (An hour with . . .), *Les Nouvelles littéraires*, 20 February 1926, *Cahiers*, no. 14.

29. *Jérôme Bardini*, p. 236.

30. Preface to *Mozart* by Annette Kolb, *Or dans la nuit* (Gold in the night), p. 73.

31. *Jérôme Bardini*, pp. 237–38.

32. *Juliette*, pp. 11–12.

33. *Siegfried et le Limousin*, p. 88.

34. "German Culture and American Universities," *Harvard Library Bulletin* 13, 1959. See Body, *Giraudoux et l'Allemagne* (Giraudoux and Germany), p. 113.

35. *Amica America*, pp. 18 and 26. See as well Body, *Giraudoux et l'Allemagne* (Giraudoux and Germany), pp. 186–87. *Amica America* comprises various texts concerning Giraudoux's diplomatic and military mission to the United States in 1917.

36. "Adieu à la guerre" (Goodbye to war), *Adorable Clio*, p. 22.

37. Raymond Schiltz, "Rencontres avec J. G." (Meetings with J. G.), *La jeunesse de J. G. en Berry* (Giraudoux's youth in Berry), records of the colloquium of Châteauroux centennial celebrations, Châteauroux (1983), p. 34.

38. Concerning "the controversy of *Siegfried*," I refer the reader to Body, *Giraudoux et l'Allemagne* (Giraudoux and Germany), pp. 292–96.

39. *Les Gracques (The Gracchi)* 1.8 (Pléiade), p. 1136. See also *La Française et la France* (The Frenchwoman and France), p. 211, and in *Intermezzo* 1.6, p. 299, "The Marseillaise of Little Girls."

40. *Pleins Pouvoirs* (Full powers), pp. 17 and 15.

41. *Les Gracques* (The Gracchi) 1.8, p. 1134.

42. *La Folle* (The Madwoman), act 2, p. 1016.

43. See especially *Pleins Pouvoirs* (Full powers), pp. 97, 194, and 199–200; *Sans pouvoirs* (Without powers), p. 194.

44. This is the title of an article written in 1934, and republished in *Or dans la nuit* (Gold in the night), p. 185.

45. *L'Ecole des Indifférents* (School for the indifferent), pp. 184 and 203.

46. *Siegfried et le Limousin*, p. 10.

47. *Pleins Pouvoirs* (Full powers), pp. 79–83.

48. *Le Temps*, 17 March 1928.

49. *Pleins Pouvoirs* (Full powers), p. 85.

50. "Discours liminaire à la charte d'Athènes" (Preface to the Athens charter) (1943), included in *Pour une politique urbaine* (For a policy of city planning) (1947), reprinted in a special edition of the *Cahiers de la Ligue urbaine et rurale*, 4th quarter (1982), p. 49.

51. *Judith* 2.4, p. 245. *Pleins Pouvoirs* (Full powers), p. 88.

52. *Visitations*, p. 79. *Visitations* contains a series of lectures on the theatre that Giraudoux delivered in Switzerland in 1942, including several previously unpublished dramatic scenes.

53. *La Folle* (The Madwoman), act 1, p. 962, and act 2, p. 997.

54. *Souvenir de deux existences* (Recollection from two existences), pp. 137–38.

55. *La Folle* (The Madwoman), act 2, p. 994.

56. Personal file in the diplomatic archives. On 5 December 1941 (*Lettres*, p. 282, "November" being an error by Giraudoux himself), he wrote to his son that Flandin had "removed him from the ministry"—which could just as well imply an invitation to retirement as an offer (which has been attested) of an ambassadorship (which was rejected). See "Les dernières années" (The final years), *Cahiers*, no. 8, pp. 23–24 and 29, as well as *Lettres*, p. 262. It will be noted that the interval is negligible between the time in which Giraudoux was supposed to be sharing an office in the Hôtel du Parc and the period in which, as a retired civil servant, he was visiting old friends in a city that had been dear to him for forty years.

57. *Lettres*, pp. 276, 278, 284, and Body, *Giraudoux et l'Allemagne* (Giraudoux and Germany), p. 434.

58. *Or dans la nuit* (Gold in the night), p. 85.

59. He had become very thin since 1941, as is evident in photographs, and possibly he had been ill for a long time: his intestines had remained delicate since the First World War. He suffered from chronic enteritis, and a touch of neurasthenia according to the American doctor who sent him back to France in 1917, and who recalled that in his youth he was athletic and muscular but not robust. His letters to Isabelle mention that he was frequently in pain.

60. See the notes of Herlin-Besson (Pléiade) p. 1720, n. 1.

61. *Les Gracques* (The Gracchi) 1.8, p. 1134.

62. *Intermezzo* 1.6, p. 295.

63. *La Folle* (The Madwoman), act 1, p. 966.

64. *Sans pouvoirs* (Without powers), p. 257. The following work is of interest, but should be read with reservations: Agnes G. Raymond, *Giraudoux devant la victoire et la défaite* (Giraudoux before victory and defeat) (Nizet, 1963), a preliminary study of the political thought of Giraudoux.

65. Martin du Gard, *Les Mémorables* (Memorabilia), vol. 3, p. 286.

66. Dawson, "De Harvard au Quai d'Orsay," p. 716.

67. Martin du Gard, *Les Mémorables* (Memorabilia), vol. 3, pp. 30 and 132.

68. André Gide, *Journal*, 30 October 1939. Gide would have this reprinted in 1942, in his *Interviews imaginaires* (Imaginary interviews): "Long live the national Revolution!"

69. See, for example, *Lettres*, p. 184.

70. "Adieu à la guerre" (Goodbye to war), *Adorable Clio*, p. 211. See my commentary in the *Revue d'histoire littéraire de la France* (September–December 1983): 869.

71. *La Française et la France* (The Frenchwoman and France), p. 30; *Pleins Pouvoirs* (Full powers), p. 175; "Armistice à Bordeaux" (Armistice in Bordeaux), *De Plains Pouvoirs à sans pouvoirs* (From full powers to without powers), p. 146; *Littérature*, pp. 307–17.

72. The character of Dumas appears to have been inspired by Achille Fournier, a childhood friend of Giraudoux, and one who would have a meteoric career in the Schneider steel works. See *Siegfried et le Limousin*, pp. 16–17, and Dawson, "De Harvard au Quai d'Orsay," p. 723, no. 77.

The character of Dumas played an even greater role in the first draft. In order to preserve (more or less!) the unity of his novel, Giraudoux deleted several dozen pages, subsequently published as "Le Signe" (The sign) and collected in *La France sentimentale* (Sentimental France). The whole of the volume *La France sentimentale* was thus made up of the overflow of diverse novels: *Siegfried et le Limousin*, *Bella*, *Jérôme Bardini*, and even *Simon*.

73. *Pleins Pouvoirs* (Full powers), pp. 138–39.

74. *Bella*, p. 221.

Conclusion

1. *Judith* 1.6, p. 220.

2. Morand, *Souvenirs de notre jeunesse* (Memories of our youth), p. 136.

3. *Siegfried et le Limousin*, p. 13.

4. "I will enjoy rereading myself because of the heaps of personal things that I have buried . . . in print. I never write books of an intimate or truly autobiographical nature. But my entire autobiography is to be found in certain minute details which are so many reference points" (interview of Giraudoux by C. Chonez, *L'Assaut*, February 1937, quoted by G. Teissier, *Cahiers de l'Association internationale des Etudes françaises*, no. 34 [May 1982]: 195).

5. The manuscript of *Souvenirs de deux existences* (Recollection from two existences) came to us in complete disorder. Regarding the published version of it (Grasset, 1975), I have expressed certain reservations in *Studi francesi*, no. 59 (1976): 265–68.

6. *Eglantine*, p. 17.

7. *Combat avec l'Ange* (Struggle with the angel), p. 15.

8. "La Grande Bourgeoise" (The upper-class woman), p. 272. Concerning Bergson, see *Amica America*. For the hardware merchant, or rather the harness maker, the carpenter, the shoemaker, see *Adorable Clio*, "Adieu à la guerre" (Goodbye to war), p. 216. "Now I will no longer fall asleep on the shoulder of a harness maker, on the heart of a carpenter. . . ." Giraudoux had accompanied Lilita to Bergson's classes, prior to meeting him, during the war, at the home of Princess Murat (Morand, *Souvenirs de notre jeunesse* [Memories of our youth], p. 80).

9. *La France sentimentale* (Sentimental France), p. 234.

10. "La Grande Bourgeoise" (The upper-class woman), p. 280.

11. *Tessa* 2.3.1, p. 1051.

12. Soupault, *Feuilles libres* (Free pages), January 1923.

13. *Pour Lucrèce* (For Lucrece) 1.6, p. 1051.

14. *Combat avec l'Ange* (Struggle with the angel), p. 315.

15. *La Menteuse* (The liar), p. 227 (1969 edition; a first edition of the six initial chapters of this posthumously published novel had appeared in 1958; chapters seven through fifteen were discovered in 1968 by Roy Prior).

BIBLIOGRAPHY

Translator's Note: The English titles of the works listed in Professor Body's bibliography appear in parentheses. The standard English language versions have been listed whenever appropriate.

Works by Jean Giraudoux

The body of Giraudoux's work is quite considerable (especially when one recalls that it was written at the same time he was pursuing a virtually uninterrupted career as a student, a civil servant, a soldier, and a statesman), a total of close to forty volumes.

The bibliography of his work is even more extensive, first of all because the majority of his writings was initially published in periodicals: his novels and short stories in magazines; his tales and articles in newspapers; his plays in *La Petite Illustration* and the *Revue de Paris*; his lectures at the University of Annals in *Conférences*, and so forth.

Conversely, diverse articles, prefaces, and lectures were collected in single volumes either while he was still living or after his death. In addition, Giraudoux nearly always modified a text between its publication in a magazine and in book form. In a small number of cases, the book itself was revised and considerably altered: *Simon the Pathetic* (1918) in 1923 and 1926, *Siegfried* (1928) in 1935, and *Judith* (1931) from the very beginning in 1931.

Finally, his principal works have appeared in numerous editions—both while Giraudoux was living and after his death.

In all, no less than 715 entries can be found in Brett Dawson's *Bibliography of the Work of Jean Giraudoux (1899–1982)* (Bellac, Association des Amis de Jean Giraudoux: 1982), 97 pp., a monument of scholarship which is indispensable for any systematic study.

The *Complete Works* is in the course of preparation for the Pléiade edition. Only the *Complete Theater* has appeared, and it is to this that page notations refer. These are preceded by an indication of the act and scene numbers, to allow the reader to consult another edition, unless of course one refers to the preface, to variants, or to early redactions.

The *Complete Works of Fiction and Cinema* will be published within the next few years. While waiting for them to appear, I refer to the most readily available editions listed in the chronological table. The reader should take into consideration not so much the date of the published edition as the number of pages. This is because in many cases, Giraudoux's works (almost all of which have now been published by Grasset) have been the object of successive printings: the date changes, but not the text or the page numbers, and our notations remain functional. In other cases, the reader must use the "rule of three" in order to derive the approximate page number that contains the passage cited or referred to.*

Finally, the index should make it easy to locate additional information given in the text or in the notes.

1909 *Provinciales* (Provincial ways), new ed. Grasset, 1922. 228 pp.

1911 *L'Ecole des Indifférents* (School for the indifferent), new ed. Grasset, 1939. 238 pp.

1917 *Lectures pour une ombre (Campaigns and Intervals)*, new ed. Grasset, 1946. 294 pp.

1918 *Simon le Pathétique* (Simon the pathetic), new ed. Grasset, 1926. 248 pp.

1918 *Amica America*, with a new preface by Jean Giraudoux. Grasset, 1938. 216 pp.

1919 *Elpénor*, new ed. Grasset, 1950. 182 pp.

1920 *Adorable Clio*. Grasset, 1939. 224 pp.

1921 *Suzanne et le Pacifique* (Suzanne and the Pacific), new ed. Grasset, 1949. 222 pp.

1922 *Siegfried et le Limousin* (Siegfried and the Limousin). Grasset, 1922. 304 pp.

1924 *Juliette au pays des hommes* (Juliette in the land of men), new ed. Grasset, 1949. 194 pp.

1926 *Bella*. Grasset, 1926. 238 pp.

1927 *Eglantine*, 58th ed. Grasset, 1949. 232 pp.

1928 *Siegfried*, a play in four acts.

1928 *Le Sport* (Sports), *Cahiers J. Giraudoux*, no. 6. Grasset, 1977. 80 pp.

1929 *Amphitryon 38*, a comedy in three acts.

1930 *Aventures de Jérôme Bardini* (The Adventures of Jerome Bardini), new ed. Grasset, 1942. 242 pp.

1930 *Fugues sur Siegfried* (Fugues on Siegfried), early drafts of the play.

---

*Translator's Note: The "rule of three" is a computation wherein the approximate page number in a variant edition may be located, as per the following example: If p. 240 is cited in an edition of 300 pages and the variant text is a volume of 200 pages, one may estimate the page number of the citation through the formula 241×200 divided by 300, or approximately p. 160.

1930 *Rues et visages de Berlin* (Streets and faces of Berlin), a text reprinted under the title *Berlin* in the collection "Ceinture du Monde" (Girdle of the world). E. Paul, 1932. 72 pp.

1931 *Judith*, a tragedy in three acts.

1932 *La France sentimentale* (Sentimental France). Grasset, 1932. 288 pp.

1933 *Intermezzo*, comedy in three acts.

1934 *Combat avec l'Ange* (Struggle with the angel), a novel. Grasset, 1934. 336 pp.

1934 *Fin de Siegfried* (End of Siegfried), an early draft of act 4.

1934 *Tessa (La Nymphe au coeur fidèle)* [Tessa (the constant nymph)], a play in three acts.

1935 *La guerre de Troie n'aura pas lieu* (Tiger at the Gates), a play in two acts.

1935 *Supplément au voyage de Cook* (Supplement to Cook's voyage), a play in one act.

1937 *Electre* (Electra), a play in two acts.

1937 *L'Impromptu de Paris* (The Paris impromptu), a play in one act.

1938 *Cantique des cantiques (Song of Songs)*, a play in one act.

1938 *Les Cinq Tentations de La Fontaine* (The five temptations of La Fontaine). Grasset, 1938. 296 pp.

1939 *Choix des Elues* (Choice of the elect), a novel. Grasset, 1939. 338 pp.

1939 *Ondine*, a play in three acts.

1939 *Pleins Pouvoirs* (Full powers). Gallimard, 1939. 216 pp.

1940. *Messages du Continental* (Adresses from the Continental Hotel). Grasset, 1940. 250 pp. (never appeared in print).

1941 *Littérature*. Grasset, 1941. 318 pp.

1942 *Le Film de la duchesse de Langeais* (The film of the duchess of Langeais), Grasset, 1942. 262 pp.

1942 *L'Apollon de Bellac (The Apollo of Bellac)*, a play in one act.

1943 *Sodome et Gomorrhe (Sodom and Gomorrah)*, a play in two acts.

1944 *Le Film de Béthanie*, text for *Les Anges du péché* (The screenplay of Bethany, text for *The angels of sin*) a screenplay by R. L. Bruckberger, Robert Bresson, and Jean Giraudoux. Paris: Gallimard, 1944. 192 pp.

1945 *La Folle de Chaillot* (*The Madwoman of Chaillot*), a play in two acts.

1947 *Visitations*. Grasset, 1952. 126 pp.

1950 *De Pleins Pouvoirs à sans pouvoirs* (From full powers to without powers), Paris: Gallimard, 1950. 272 pp.

1951 *La Française et la France* (not Giraudoux's title) [The Frenchwoman and France], Paris: Gallimard, 1951. 248 pp.

1952 *Les Contes d'un Matin* (Tales for a morning), introduced by Laurent Le Sage, Paris: Gallimard, 1952. 174 pp.

1953 *Pour Lucrèce* (*For Lucrece*), a play in three acts.

1958 *Les Gracques* (The Gracchi), an unfinished play.

1958 *Oeuvres littéraires diverses* (Assorted literary works), a single-volume anthology, first edition limited to 5,765 copies. Grasset. 830 pp.

1969 *La Menteuse* (*The Liar*), Grasset, 1969. 282 pp.

1975 *Lettres*, edited, collected, and annotated by Jacques Body. Klincksieck, Publications of the Sorbonne, 1975. 284 pp.

1975 *Souvenir de deux existences* (Recollection from two existences). Grasset, 1975. 144 pp.

1982 *Théâtre complet* (Complete theater). Preface by Jean-Pierre Giraudoux. General introduction by Jacques Body. Edition published under the direction of Body in collaboration with Marthe Herlin-Besson, Etienne Brunet, Brett Dawson, Janine Delort, Lise Gauvin, Gunnar Graumann, Wayne Ready, Jacques Robichez, Guy Teissier, and Colette Weil. Paris: Gallimard, 1982. 856 pp., Pléiade edition.

1985 *Enquêtes et interviews I (1919–1931)* [Studies and interviews I (1919–1931)], *Cahiers*, no. 14.

Studies of the Work of Jean Giraudoux

The reader may find useful the bibliographies already extant, which appear at the end of the following works:

Albérès, René Marill. *Esthétique et morale chez Jean Giraudoux* (Aesthetics and morality in the work of Jean Giraudoux). Nizet, 1957. Organized by subject.

Body, Jacques. *Giraudoux et l'Allemagne* (Giraudoux and Germany). Didier-Erudition, 1975. Organized alphabetically; this one is more current than the former.

For a systematic study, one will find a nearly comprehensive list in the following group of volumes:

Anamur, Hasan. *Bibliographie chronologique des publications de langue française sur Jean Giraudoux et son oeuvre de 1909 à 1970* (A chronological bibliography of the French language publications on Jean Giraudoux and his work from 1909 to 1970). Ankara: Ankara Universitesi Basimevi, 1980.

Le Sage, Laurent. *L'oeuvre de Jean Giraudoux*, vol. 2 (books and articles concerning Giraudoux). State College, Pa.: Pennsylvania State University Press, 1958.

Le Sage gives an abstract of each article and also several indices. On the other hand, Anamur is somewhat more comprehensive, and covers the years up to 1970, while Le Sage ends in 1955.

These two bibliographical works are available only at the Association des amis de Jean Giraudoux, 1 rue Louis-Jouvet, 87300 Bellac.

Finally, the Association des amis de Jean Giraudoux has published annually since 1972 the *Cahiers Jean Giraudoux* (Grasset), which conclude with a bibliography of the preceding year, and which themselves include numerous unpublished or forgotten texts of Jean Giraudoux and numerous studies of the writer, his work, and his period.

Works Most Frequently Cited in the Present Study

BIOGRAPHICAL STUDIES

Aucuy, Jean-Marc. *La jeunesse de Giraudoux, souvenirs de Marc Aucuy* (Giraudoux's youth, memories of Marc Aucuy), compiled by his son. Paris: Spid, 1948. 174 pp.

Giraudoux, Jean-Pierre. *Le fils* (The son). Grasset, 1967. 312 pp. In this semiautobiographical novel, the son of the author, himself a writer (he is the author of another *Electra* and an *Amphitryon*, not 38 but 39, among other works), has interpolated some memories of his father, memories that he has also relived in the foreward to *Théâtre complet* (Complete theater). New ed. in Livre de poche, 1985.

Morand, Paul. *Giraudoux. Souvenirs de notre jeunesse* (Giraudoux: Memories of our youth), letters and unpublished documents. Geneva: La Palatine, 1948. 158 pp. This work concludes with an "Adieu to Giraudoux," which was initially conceived as an address to the students of a French Institute abroad. As a result, it summarizes all that precedes it, in a somewhat raccharine style; but with the addition of a few key details. The first part, on the other hand, is very lively, very rich, and very precise. Reprinted in *Mon plaisir en littérature* (My favorite authors). Paris: Gallimard, 1982. Idées, no. 464. 372 pp.

GENERAL STUDIES

Albérès, René Marill. *Esthétique et morale chez Jean Giraudoux* (Aesthetics and morality in the work of Jean Giraudoux). Nizet, 1957. 570 pp. (detailed table of contents, index of proper names, and index of Giraudoux's characters).

Body, Jacques. *Jean Giraudoux et l'Allemagne* (Jean Giraudoux and Germany). Didier, 1975. 522 pp. (The index is unfortunately incorrect: after p. 328, add two page numbers.)

Høst, Gunnar. *L'oeuvre de Jean Giraudoux*. Oslo: H. Aschehoug, 1942. 250 pp.

Pizzorusso, Arnold. *Tre Studi su Giraudoux* (Three studies of Giraudoux). Florence: Sansoni, 1954. 196 pp.

STUDIES ON GIRAUDOUX'S THEATER

Robichez, Jacques. *Le théâtre de Giraudoux*. Société d'édition d'enseignement supérieur, 1976. 290 pp.

Of the three American monographs (written in English), we recommend:

Le Sage, Laurent. *Jean Giraudoux. His Life and Works.* Pennsylvania State University Press, 1959, 240 pp., which is based on original research.

Reilly, John H. *Jean Giraudoux.* Boston, Twayne P., 1978, which uses recent studies.

INDEX

This selective index seeks to highlight the essential moments and themes in the life and work of Jean Giraudoux. Proper names of those who knew him or who have written about him are in roman letters; titles of works are in *italics*; names of places, which he visited or wrote about, are in CAPITAL LETTERS; and the themes of his work and of the present study are in **boldface**.

Abreu (Lilita), 85–89, 118
Abreu (Pierre), 85, 118
Adams (Mr. and Mrs.), 82, 134n
Adorable Clio, 20, 28, 56, 107, 109, 118, 122n, 123n, 138n, 140n
Adventures of Jerome Bardini (The), 41, 45, 72–73, 76, 82, 94, 107, 109, 131n, 132n, 134n, 136n, 138n, 140n
Albalat (Antoine), 17
Albeaux-Fernet (Michel), 90
Albérès (René Marill), 12, 20, 65, 134n, 135n
AMERICA, 18, 22, 43, 44, 92
Amica America, 28, 44, 46, 109, 125n, 126n, 138n
Amnesia, 76
Amphitryon 38, 11–12, 64, 123n
Angels of Sin, 80
Animals, 75, 132n
Anouilh (Jean), 11
Apollo of Bellac (The), 12, 39, 64, 68, 79, 97, 98, 108, 130n, 133n, 136n, 138n
Aragon (Louis), 13, 45, 115
ARRAS, 44, 94
ASIA, 43–44
Aucuy (Jean-Marc), 66, 70, 130n

BAGHDAD, 43
Bailly (Louis), 22
Barthlélemy (Maurice), 135n, 136n
BAULE (LA), 44
Bayard (Pierre), 19, 58
Bella, 10, 27, 54, 56, 63, 129n, 140n
BELLAC, 29, 31, 34–41

Béraud (Henri), 93, 135n
Bergson (Henri), 109, 121, 140n
BERLIN, 43, 44, 81
Bernardin de Saint-Pierre, 54
Berthelot (Philippe), 10, 22, 54, 90, 127n
BESSINES, 35, 39
Beucler (André), 65, 105, 129n, 130n, 137n
Billy (André), 17, 18
Bourdet (Denise), née Rémon, 81
Bourdet (Edouard), 81
Boylesve (Mr. and Mrs. René), 87
Brasillach (Robert), 115
Bressy (Pierre), 21, 33, 43, 103–4, 117, 129n
Breton (André), 47–48
Brun (Louis), 23–24, 26
Brunet (Etienne), 13, 53, 60, 127n, 129n
Bunau-Varilla (Maurice), 25, 29–30, 115, 118

Caillaux (Joseph), 115
CALIFORNIA, 43–45
Campaigns and Intervals, 26, 28, 125n
CAP-FERRAT, 44
Career in diplomacy, 10, 42–44, 50–51, 64–65, 103–5, 109, 117
CÉRILLY, 23, 35, 39
Chateaubriand (François-Auguste-René), 54
CHÂTEAUROUX, 39 (See also LYCÉE)
Chénier (André), 54

Choice of the Elect, 41, 58, 127n, 129n
Cicero, 54
City planning, 12, 32, 111–13, 119
Claudel (Paul), 10, 54, 126n, 135n
Clermont (Emile), 17
Commissioner General of Information, 9, 65, 104–5, 108, 109, 117
Constant (Benjamin), 54
Cordelier(s), 62, 81, 92, 134n
Corneille (Pierre), 38
Couple (the), 98, 100–102
CUBA, 43, 85
CUSSET, 35, 85

Daladier (Edouard), 117
Daragnès, 90
DARDANELLES, 43, 91–92
Daudet (Alphonse), 69–70
Daudet (Léon), 24
Dawson (Brett), 122n, 124n, 135n, 138n, 157n
Death, 115–16
Diderot (Denis), 54
Doumic (René), 110
Dubech (Lucien), 110
Du Bos (Charles), 87
Duchâteau (Gédéon), 70, 78
Durry (Marie-Jeanne), 11, 67, 130

Ecole Normale Supérieure, 17, 42, 48–50, 52, 64, 66
Education (elementary), 48–49
Education (secondary), 47, 48, 51–53
Education (higher), 48, 49, 52
Eglantine, 27–28, 40, 41
Electra, 21, 56, 57, 64, 66, 99, 101, 107, 114, 123n, 128n, 130n, 132n, 133n, 138n
Elpenor, 10–11, 36, 57, 66, 73, 76–77, 122n, 125n, 127n, 131n, 132n
Emile-Paul Brothers, 25, 27, 124n
Escape, 41, 42, 44–45, 105

Feminism, 99–100
Fénelon, 39
Figaro (Le), 55, 111, 112, 115
Five Temptations of La Fontaine (The), 38–39, 74, 75, 132n
For Lucrece, 12, 64, 98–99, 101, 129n
Foreign lands, 11, 39, 42–46
Frenchwoman and France (The), 99, 137n, 140n

Freud (Sigmund), 33, 73–74
Friendship, 81–83
Full Powers, 12, 22, 33, 110–13, 119, 138n, 139n, 140n

Gaity, 61
Gallimard (Gaston), 87
Games, 62–68, 77
Gaulle (Charles de), 106, 114, 116
Genette (Gérard), 57, 128n, 129n
GENEVA, 41, 42
Gide (André), 10, 20, 28–29, 118, 124n, 140n
Giraudoux (Alexandre, brother of Jean Giraudoux), 44, 78–79
Giraudoux (Anne, called Antoinette, née Lacoste, mother of Jean Giraudoux), 30, 35, 44, 62, 78–79
Giraudoux (Jean-Pierre, son of Jean Giraudoux), 19, 92, 96–97, 106, 115, 121, 136n
Giraudoux (Léon, father of Jean Giraudoux), 34, 42, 78–79, 90
Giraudoux (Suzanne, née Boland, wife of Jean Giraudoux), 89–93, 94–98, 123n
Goebbels, 117, 118
Gold in the Night, 125n, 127n, 128n, 135n, 137n
Gracchi (The), 43, 110–11, 116
Grasset (Bernard), 23–28
Great people of the world (the), 55–57

HARVARD UNIVERSITY, 17, 39, 42, 44, 55, 81, 85, 109
Haviland (Paul and Suzanne, née Lalique), 35, 81
Hébertot (Jacques), 62
Hébreu (Léon), 82
Herlin-Besson (Marthe), 139n
Herriot (Edouard), 128n
Heymann (Lucie), 123n, 136n
Hitler (Adolf), 56
Hofmannsthal (Hugo von), 110
HONFLEUR, 44
Hugo (Victor), 82, 115

Imagination, 106–7, 118–19
Intermezzo, 20, 37, 40, 41, 45–46, 60, 73, 74, 97, 99, 106–7, 108, 116, 129n, 131n, 136n, 138n, 139n

Isabelle (mistress of Jean Giraudoux), 95–98
ISTANBUL, 43

Jewish controversy, 31–34
Joubert (Joseph), 54
Jouvet (Louis), 18, 98, 116
Judith, 32, 41, 57, 64, 65, 67–68, 84, 100, 124n, 130n, 134n, 137n
Juliette in the Land of Men, 27, 40, 41, 59, 72, 75–76, 129n, 131n, 132n
Jung (C. G.), 73

Labonne (Eirik), 81
Lacoste (Giraudoux's maternal family), 34–35, 78–80, 103, 114–15
La Fontaine (Jean de), 35, 38–39
Lalique (Suzanne), SEE Haviland
Lalou (René), 65
Lamartine (Alphonse de), 38, 82, 101
La Motte-Fouqué (Friedrich de), 57
Language (French), 34, 52–53
Larbaud (Valery), 40
"Last Dream of Edmond About" (The), 30
Lavisse (Ernest), 55, 125n, 126n
Lefèvre (Frédéric), 66, 123n, 124n, 127n, 130n, 138n
Legend, 50, 121
Léger (Alexis), 104
Le Sage (Laurent), 124n, 136n
Lettres, 123n, 125n, 128n, 129n, 133n, 134n, 135n, 139n
LIMOUSIN, 31, 44–46, 124n
Littérature, 115, 125n, 127n, 129n, 131n, 132n, 138n, 140n
Love, 82–102
LYCÉE OF CHÂTEAUROUX, 17, 21, 49, 51, 52, 63, 68–70
LYCÉE LAKANAL, 17, 48, 49, 52–53

Madero (Anita de), 93–96
Madwoman of Chaillot (The), 12, 30, 64, 98, 101, 106, 111, 114, 116, 136n, 138n, 139n
Maiden of Chamignoux (The), 133n
Mallarmé (Stéphane), 42, 54
Manière (Jean-Emmanuel), 29–30
Mann (Heinrich), 110
Maria Chapdelaine, 24–25, 27
Marivaux (Pierre Carlet de), 54
Marker (Chris), 50, 65, 123n, 126n

Martin du Gard (Maurice), 62, 129n, 139n, 140n
Matin (Le), 25, 30
Mauron (Charles), 67, 73, 130n, 131n
Middle Ages, 54, 128n
Morand (Eugène), 22, 81
Morand (Paul), 18, 22, 42–43, 64, 81, 84, 88, 90, 92, 95, 117, 118, 120, 133n, 134n, 135n, 136n, 140n
Moréas (Jean), 17
Moreau (Michel), 124n, 125n
Morize (André), 18
Mozart, 109, 138
MUNICH, 17, 39, 44, 55, 81, 128n
Music, 66–67
Musset (Alfred de), 38

Name (Jean Giraudoux), 29–30
Narcissus, 72
Nationalism, 34, 45–46, 109–10
Nerval (Gérard de), 74, 76
NEW YORK, 42, 43, 44, 45
"Night in Châteauroux," 10, 138n

Ondine, 11, 41, 57, 61, 64, 95, 100, 101, 104, 108, 122n, 129n, 133n, 136n, 137n, 138n
Painting, 22
PARIS, 39, 41–42, 112
Paris Impromptu (The), 52, 56, 77, 108, 132n, 138n
Péguy (Charles), 22
PELLEVOISIN, 35, 39
Pétain (Philippe), 114, 116, 124n
Philipe (Gérard), 98
Philippe (Charles-Louis), 23, 40, 125n
Pierrefeu (Jean de), 17
Pineau (Christian), 90
Pioch (Georges), 45
Pizzorusso (Arnaldo), 124n
Plaideux (Hugues), 132n
Plants, 75, 132n
Pliny, 55
Poincaré (Raymond), 43, 104, 118
Polignac (Charles de), 88, 118
Politics (French), 33–34, 105–6, 110–13
PORTUGAL, 43, 44, 92
Pride, 31, 108–9
Prometheus, 58
Proust (Marcel), 10, 13, 17, 25, 28, 29, 40, 81, 124n

Provincial Ways, 10, 20, 22, 24, 25, 28, 35, 39, 42, 80, 82, 83, 122n, 125n, 133n, 134n
Pseudonyms, 29–30
Psychoanalysis, 70–71, 73–75
Purity, 32, 76

Quintillian, 54

Racine, 54, 76, 120, 134n
Racism, 31–34, 48
Ratel (Simone), 128n
Raymond (Agnes), 52, 139n
Renan (Ernest), 48, 75
Renard (Jules), 40
Restif de la Bretonne, 54
Rimbaud (Arthur), 54
Ripert (Emile), 123n
Robichez (Jacques), 11, 122n, 128n, 129n
Roosevelt (Theodore), 55
Rousseau (Jean-Jacques), 54

SAINT-AMAND-MONTROND, 35, 39, 79–80, 103
Saint-John Perse, SEE Léger
Salmon (André), 17
SAN FRANCISCO, 43, 44
Sartre (Jean-Paul), 9, 32, 65, 95, 109, 136n
School for the Indifferent, 12, 36, 44, 80, 123n, 131n, 133n, 134n
Secret, 9–10, 73–75
Sénancour (Etienne Pivert de), 54
Sentimental France, 38–39, 124n, 125n, 131n, 140n
Service (military), 42, 43, 50–51
Sévigné (Madame de), 54
Siegfried (play), 11, 19, 20, 30, 45, 71, 110, 123n, 125n, 128n, 130n, 131n, 132n, 135n, 138n
Siegfried and the Limousin (novel), 20, 24, 27, 29, 38, 40, 44–45, 81, 86, 93, 99, 118, 125n, 134n, 135n, 137n, 138n, 140n
Silence, 75, 121
Simon the Pathetic, 10, 18, 21, 30, 45, 47, 52, 56, 61, 69–72, 79, 82, 84, 88–90, 108, 122n, 123n, 124n, 125n, 126n, 127n, 128n, 129n, 130n, 131n, 133n, 134n, 135n, 138n, 140n

Sluice gates, 131n
Sodom and Gomorrah, 12, 57, 62, 64, 98, 101–2, 114, 123n, 136n, 137n
Song of Songs, 12, 41, 44, 100, 137n
Soupault (Philippe), 47, 48, 121, 123n, 126n, 141n
SOUTH PACIFIC, 39, 43–44, 58
Sports, 22, 99, 136–37n
Sports, 22
Staël (Madame de), 54
Struggle with the Angel, 56, 57, 94, 136n
Suffering, 67–71
Supplement to Cook's Voyage, 12, 79, 128–29n, 133n, 137n
Surrealism, 47–48, 57
Suzanne and the Pacific, 11, 20, 28, 36–37, 41, 48, 57, 91, 122n, 125n, 127n, 135n

Tacitus, 55
Tadié (Jean-Yves), 124n
TEHRAN, 43
Teissier (Guy), 124n, 135n
Tessa, 137n, 141n
Tharaud (J. and J.), 17
Tiger at the Gates, 10, 57, 72, 99, 100–101, 105, 127n, 130n, 131n, 137n
TIMOR, 58
Toulet (Paul-Jean), 17
Toulouse (family), 64, 80, 129n
Tournier (Michel), 11, 119, 122n

Valéry (Paul), 10
Vallette (Alfred), 23
VICHY (Allier), 35, 62, 114–15
Vichy (government), 32, 114–15, 117
Vigny (Alfred de), 79, 82, 128n
Visitations, 64, 129n, 139n
Vuillard (Edouard), 18

War (1914–18), 43, 47, 51, 74, 90–92, 117
War (1939–45), 44, 96–98, 104–6, 114–16
Weil (Colette), 20, 126n, 133n, 136n
Wilson (Woodrow), 56
Without Powers, 97, 109, 139n, 140n
Women, 12, 78–102
Writing, 17–23, 28–29

Youth, 34–35, 40–41, 45–50, 59